I welcome you to the wonder of unraveling one's conditioning.

Peeling back the layers, I came to explore what it means to be authentic to oneself. As I walk the path of food addiction recovery, I am beginning to understand that most of what I am tearing down isn't a sickness, disease, or biochemical disposition. It is deeper; I am dismantling conditioning. The life I was born into came with a price tag. The price was autonomy.

Though doughy and soft, I live like an Olympic athlete in the emotional body. This striving has been going on since the day I arrived. I was constantly trying to get onto the podium to claim my gold medal of belonging. The award symbolizes my success in finally breathing my first breath as a sovereign human being. Not my mother's daughter or the wide-eyed obedient child everyone molded me to be.

Each bit of healing I do inside my inner landscape is a gift of health to the lands I live and walk upon. The future generations I tend in my family and relationships. These Love letters are a gesture of goodwill to the Earth that holds and shapes my vitality. Our vitality.

In service,
Brigid

Love Letters to The Earth Vol 2

Conditions of Conditioning

Brigid Hopkins

ISBN: 979-8-9857324-1-2

Cover Design by: Nskvsky's

Formatting by: Michael Davie - grimhousepub.com/plans-pricing

Contents

1+1 = 3

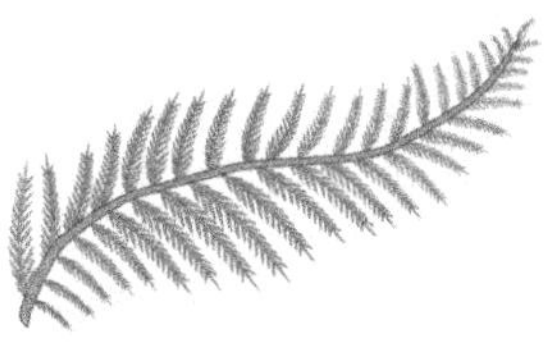

Before there was us
It was you
Two separate beings
Not considering their
Legacy

You had lives to live
Trials to wade
Memories in the making

Then came two
Two fractals wishing to be
Whole
Carrying the burdens
Of unmet dreams
Fantasy
Lust
And greed
You wanted fun
Not longevity

One plus one
Equals three
A bouncy ball of responsibility
Dreams a distant memory

Fragments creating resistance
Of how to care for little me

Three became two
Carrying the tattered threads
Of unmet needs
Loves fading memory
A world of demands
Carted by expectation
Of how to live acceptably

She needed you
So did I
We would wander through the days
Wondering why you didn't choose us
Why one became three, then two
Who are you
Where did you go

The drama sure to unfold
Can you outrun regret
The little three
Is now me

I picked up the baton
Of our Ancestry
No more hiding
No more denying
Our humanity

Every part of you created me
Beats within my cells
The trials

Struggles
Misunderstandings
The love

Love will see us through
Me, Us, Them and you
The power to forgive ripples through
Space and time
Healing infinitely
What couldn't be spoken
Is no longer broken
In my psychology

Our hearts are strong
Our history rewritten
I am not the bastard child of lust
I came from the stars to turn
Dust into diamonds
Illuminating our legacy

All I see is Them

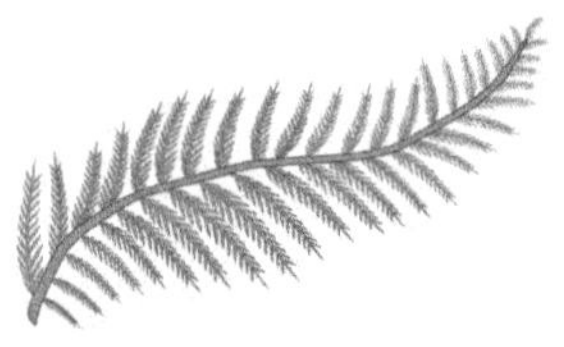

You know them
The ones who say:

You can't
You won't
It is best not to try
You're never going anywhere
You're not good enough
You're too slow
You're too fat
You're poor
You're weak
You're too skinny
You're a different race
You're the wrong gender

You know them
They live in every country, state, city, school, office, and the like
They are everywhere
They are us

We grew up hearing it. If not directly. Then around town.
If not spoken directly, then it was implied.

I hear them when I go to speak to my children.
I hear them when I look in the mirror.
I hear them when I go for a new job.
I hear them when I fall.
I hear them when I am scared.

Now hear me!

That voice has taken up enough space in my mind,
heart, and spirit.
They may never know the effect they had on my life.
But it stops right here, right now, today.
I am taking back my right.
To think my thoughts without judgment.
To say what I need to communicate with mindful
consideration
I am here to live freely
Be compassionate
Take my time
Move at my own pace
Walk my stride
Take my risks
Love freely
Think freely
Live freely
Be as weird
Far out
And different as I CHOOSE to be for me
I am not imposing on you
I am exposing me
Know the difference
I have the right to breathe
I have the right to live

As I choose to be

I am slowly becoming them, and the them I choose to be supports humanity doing life differently.

Breaking the restrictions of our
CONDITIONING

Ascension

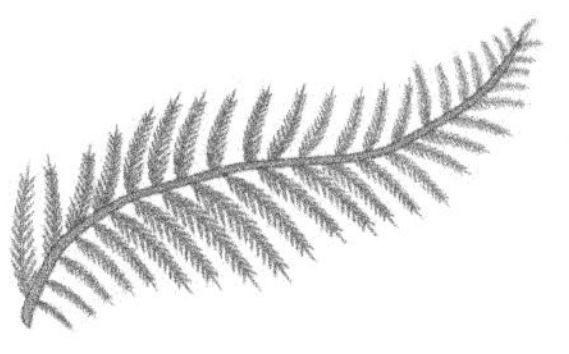

With emphasis on
Love
Light
Ascension
High Vibes
Tribes
And
Responsibility

After a big expansion
Comes the inevitable
Retraction

It can leave one feeling
A little
Less certainty
When deflated

It feels dense
Small
Isolating

Am I ok
To show up
When I feel this way

Will I detract high vibes
And ascent
When I feel like a
Shriveled balloon
Left to dry on cement

It's all a part of the process
No one more right than the other
They are cycles of growth
We all go through
When feeling and attentive
To the life moving through us

Be the puffy balloon
The shriveled balloon
The air in between

After all this life
It is one of many
Dreams

Asking for More

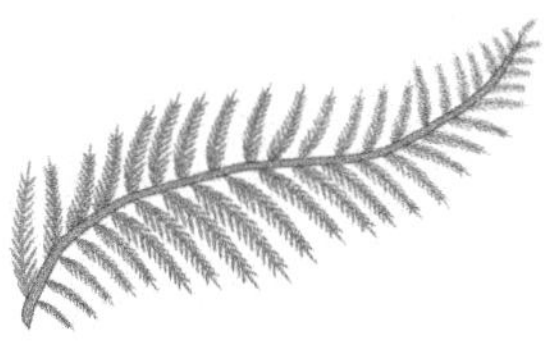

I wish to touch the milky way.
Not with eyes alone, the nothingness that glows from
deep inside my bones.

You give me more than I can receive
And yet, I'm here once again asking for more

Fill me
Empty me
Wash me clean
Stretch me
Wring me
Hold me

Tell me I'm worth it
Desires count for something
My numbness Dulls my taste for this
Existence

I long to hold your hand
Spin in the colorless dust
Of expansiveness
The place that has yet to be born
Through atoms that

Were spit and hurled
With a furious nature
By which alchemy transfers
A past washed clean
Through fire and friction

Aspirations

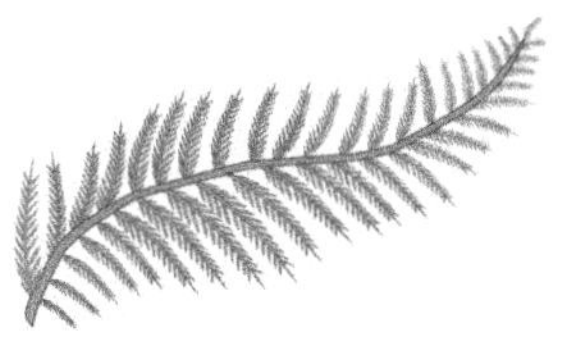

To meet the famous ones
The rich
The successful
The esteemed

Mean that I am one of them too.

Is that true?

Can I claim my provenance based on those I know?
What do they exemplify?
Why do I try
To be like them?

Where in their sheen
Is the real me?

Do I care how many followers I have?
Who I influence
Who idolizes me?

Is that why I am here
What am I meant to do?

What about the quiet moments

Of bliss
And ecstasy?

The moments that no one else sees
Does that make me lesser than
When I am the quiet wind over the land

This mixed-up society
Places fame
Over
Dignity

Praise
Over
Repose

Maybe it's my delusion
That obscures
The juxtapose
Being a no one to some
And everything to none.

Be a Container, not a Sieve

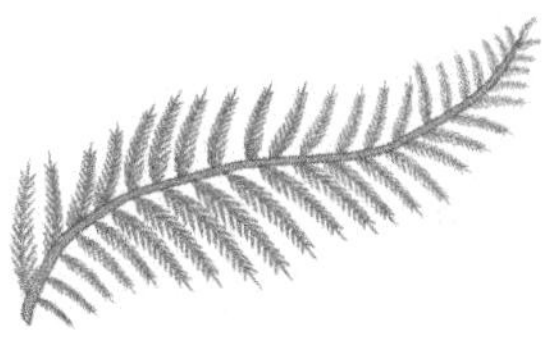

I see the power of vulnerability in a new way.

The intoxicating effect it can have over the listener they are not aware of during the experience.

When a person is entirely vulnerable, they can appear fragile at times.

As the listener and holder of the container, great care needs to be kept in the forefront of how you hold the person's space.

The truth is, they are not broken or wounded.
They are breaking open, peeling back the skin of their seed.

Allow them the space to take root for their greater purpose.

As the observer of the process, it is paramount not to get entangled in the power and intensity of the moment.

For the giver, it is fleeting.

For the observer, it can be empowering, which is a false sense of power.

It's so essential only to hold the container.

Kindly put a lid on all that was shared hand it back because the giver only deserves that empowerment for themselves!

Before I forgot

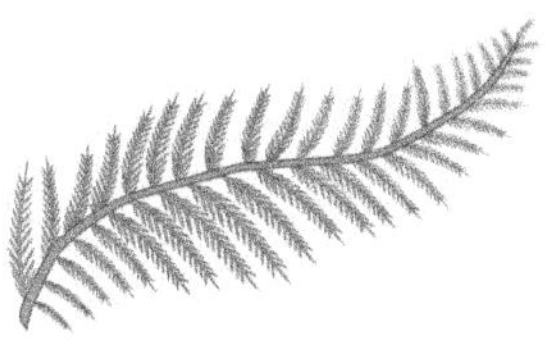

Who was I before I forgot?
I was the girl that would roll in the fields.
I was the girl that would run around naked, laughing
with the sun.
I was the girl that believed in fairies and the hidden
worlds that no one else could see.
I was the girl who believed in all humanity's goodness
before she was given reasons to question it.
I was the girl who knew what she came here to deliver
before her brilliance dulled by the murk of other
people's insecurities.
I was the girl who would chase rainbows.
I was the girl who would dance in the puddles left by
the storm.
I was the girl who could see the hidden worlds in the
clouds, hearing the whispers of the Ancestors in the
wind.

I am that girl, she was never lost.
A temporary forgetting.

She's the pulse in my veins—the beats in my heart.
She's the drummer by which I follow all of my bold
steps.
She is accepting, unconditionality, agenda-less.

She is love. I am her. She is me.
We are.

Blemishes

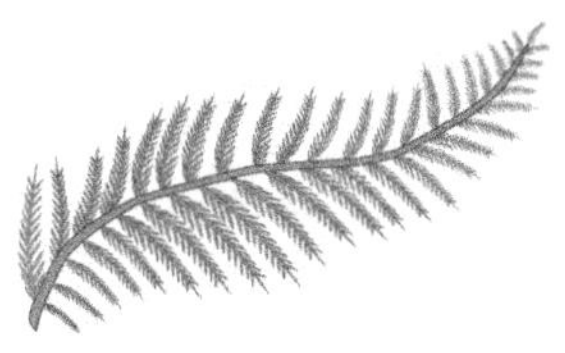

The mirror went black
Stop it!
Stop it right now!

Stop what?

Stop looking for what is wrong
Stop looking with yesterday's eyes
The eyes of your peers
Your family
Your mentors

Stop looking for what isn't there
Anything you see is either
Memory
Or
Creation

Stop looking for blemishes
Fat
Blemishes
Scars

How do you know that's what I'm doing?

I see it in your eyes
I feel it in your sigh
I know it's the way showed to you

Mirrors aren't for vanity
They're for clarity

Clarifying
Fog
Distortion
Misrepresentation
Misunderstanding

Stop looking in the mirror for what isn't there
There's nothing wrong in your appearance
Your feelings

Your emotions
Are another kind of mirror

None of them rule your domain unless you believe it to be true.

So tell me
Who are you?
This moment
How does this you walk, talk, and present themself in the world outside of you?

What do you want me to see when I look at you?

Clean up anything that doesn't reflect that.

Be good to yourself and know the mirror isn't here to
hurt you.
It's here to clarify what had.

Catch your Shadow

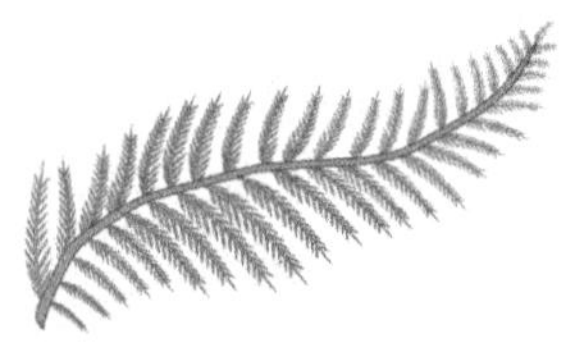

Stop
Turn
Catch your shadow
The loyal companion
In your periphery
Wondering if you'll
Accept her divinity

Gaze upon the infinite
You possess
Not in the distance
Remembrance

The generations
Lay the ground
For you to be found
Whole

Be their space in your bones
That wonder
What you don't know
Let it fill
Be distilled by your
Codes of inheritance

Children

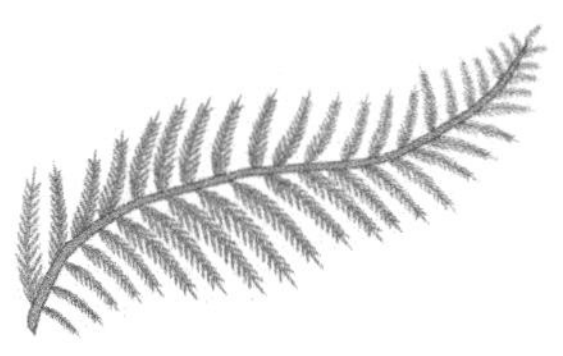

The years float by
Haze covers Molly's eyes
Once young and spry
She's now a senior
As I listen to you giggle
I don't know why
Your face is hidden behind the laptop
Our worlds close and far apart
All of the moments I said; "just one more minute"
Never meant anything
Those minutes are gone
I long to reclaim every second
Soon you'll be driving
Hanging with your friends
No longer looking to me as your idle
Now I am human
Flawed
You might even say annoying
No more cleaning scraped knees
Blowing on bee stings
These ebbs and flows
That blow through our home
My heart
Airing the grief
Moments of Confusion

Sorrow
I would take it all back
Begin again
And
I'd still tell myself I did it wrong
Because you only see with clarity
When you are farther down the road
I love you, my children
Our hearts are forever woven
I may not be perfect
But I am honest
I have always loved you full out
Even when it was a mess
This is life
We strive and fall
Never surrender
Let the grief come
Wash away the stains
Motherhood is difficult
Tender and raw
I would do it a thousand times over
Catching myself when I fall
You see it all
There's no hiding
No pretending
A house full of personalities
Learning
Forgiving
And growing
Creating promises today
That bloom tomorrow
Improving our lineage
One generation to the next

Like a delicate nest
If placed just so, the winds will come
Strands will blow
The remains rebuilt by the broods
Of tomorrow

Clarify the Lens

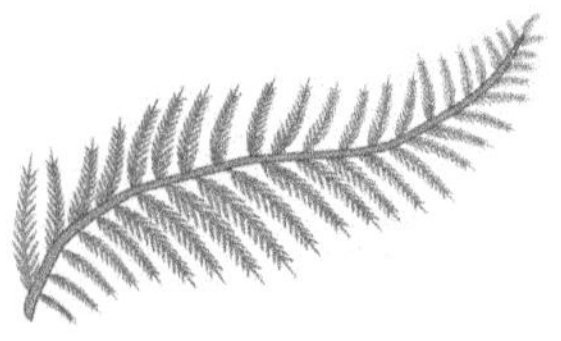

I'm not who I say I am

I SAY I'm not enough
I'm just a mom
I'm only a homemaker
I'm invisible
I'm inarticulate
I'm unattractive
I've no personality
I'm not kind
I'm not worthy
I'm not smart
I'm not talented
I've nothing to offer

I'm not who I say I am

I'm MORE

I am brave

I am a caretaker

I am raising leaders

I am dedicated to service

I am brilliant

I am humble

I am nurturing

I am funny

I am a warrior

I am witty

I am loving

I am relentless

I am fierce

I am compassionate

I am a leader

I am strong

I am fearless

I am charismatic

I am not who I SAY I am

Time to change the record

Embrace
The song of who I deny myself
To be
Welcome these qualities fully
Into me

Conditioned Conditioning

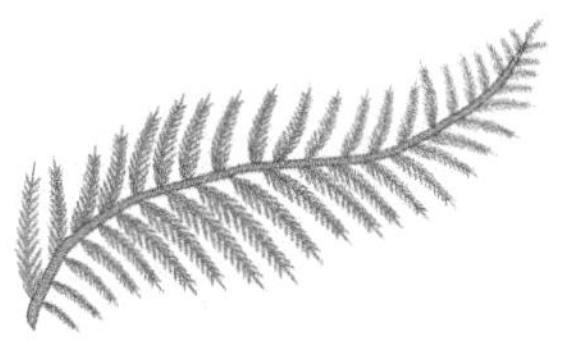

My hunch is conditioning started because someone felt unsafe

Rules
Conditions
Limitations
Restrictions
Impositions

All to regain a sense of safety
All the while, the effect was traumatizing for all who were inflicted by these regulations
They stopped man being free
Enslaving all to poverty

You can't have wealth
If your violence imprisons
Conditioning is a silent killer
We have all been served

Confessions of a Giver

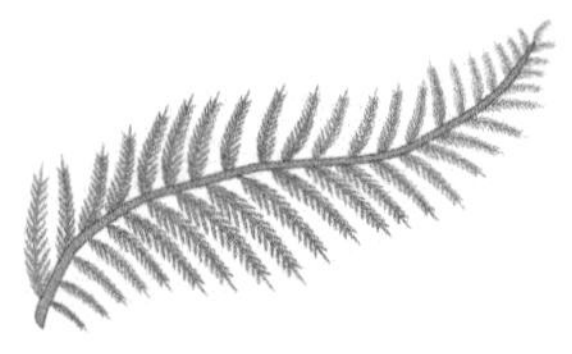

Confessions of a giver.

Giving is my primary love language

At least it's what I've most curated

It brings me great joy to give

I put time and effort into considering the receiver
If it doesn't feel right, I wait
I don't give to say I gave

Nor do I expect anything in return

It's done with great care

And...

I have put so much time and energy into giving that I'm a fawn as a receiver.
Receiving is not well-walked terrain.

Some things take time for me to receive.
I've conditioned myself to be closed off to the attention of others.

Receiving means you see me.

You see a part of me, and you wish for me to know I am seen.

My light. My Divine nature.

It takes time for me to receive your good intentions
Could you not give up on me? I am opening. I am learning. I am trusting. I am allowing. I am surrendering to the messengers being led to me. I listen as often and long as I can, even going past my edges.

Please be patient and know it's not in gest. Sometimes it takes me a few minutes, others times days or more. But I eventually received it.

My defenses have been active longer than my guardians. It's a process.

I am walking the roads leading me to good souls like you. The ones who mean me no harm. Who creates space for me to uncoil.

Receiving all you offer me leaves me feeling delicate, vulnerable, exposed. It's a beautiful view from here. I am receiving in the ways I can while stretching into new areas I didn't know was possible.

Thank you

Creation vs. Stagnation

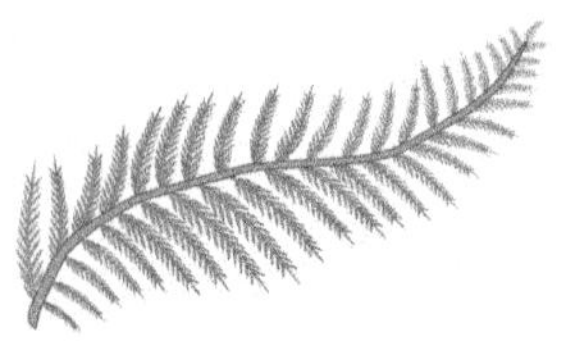

Creation versus stagnation.
When we want to make changes in our lives, we often have an idea of what we want to go after.

The missing key that we don't usually know is how it will feel for us to have something that we've never had before as we take steps to change the habits that have us where we are.

We rely a lot on the old stories.
But when we're in the state of creation, there isn't a story; it's all experiential raw, unfiltered, uncut information.

I use the word unfiltered loosely because we are constantly filtering.

However, be aware that if you're telling a story, you're not in the space of creation.

You're not in a new state; you're in a fixed state of what was.

Development

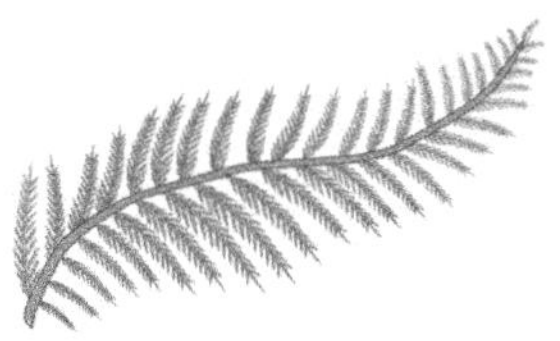

You are the mother
The egg
The developing baby
At any age
You're still developing
It's a constant trial
Of life
And
Death
Go easy
Let love keep you warm
Let life slowly turn you over
Inside
And out
Grace knows you
You are learning to know
Thyself
Keep your skin supple
Your feathers stiff
You're learning to spread
Your wings
To soar
Glide on the winds
Twirl

And dive
Is what it means
To be alive

Dimmer Switch

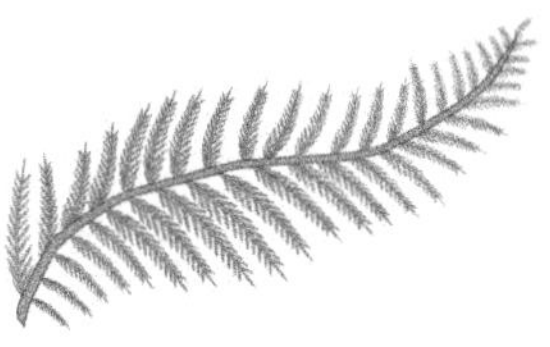

Let me illustrate how skilled you truly are, at skirting around your brilliance.

You don't make the call you need to build your website.

You've baked another dozen cookies for the kids you're planning to have down the road.

You've slept in until noon and missed booking the trip of your dreams, again. Tomorrow is another day.

You ignore the fourth call from your aunt who is trying hard to deliver a handsome donation to your cause.

You have ignored the handsome cashier, even after you swore you'd make this your year of flirting.

This is your life. These moments are yours. No one. I mean, no one can convince you.
Sell you.
Or organize your priorities.

The Universe is trying to support you. Give you what you need, when you need it. AND it takes your participation to be available to receive.

You're spectacular at disrupting your possibility because.....

It's all bullshit! All of it.

There are no more minutes to spare on believing your dimmer switch.

Turn this truck around and be blinded by your brilliance. Yes, you.

You are EVERYTHING! Stop forsaking your gold to the brass that is weighing your dreams down.

Discontent

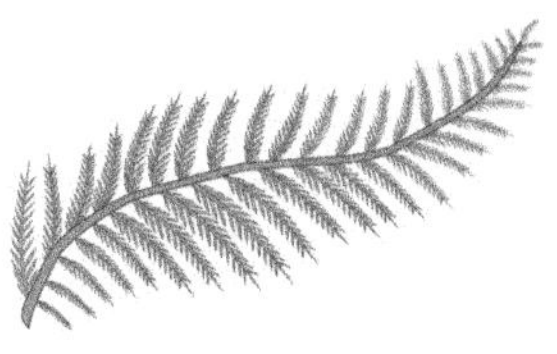

The model of how to live is breaking down.

Oppression was once a fixed notion.
Approved of and supported.
Slowly crumbling.

Make no mistake, the in-between is just as frightening.

Who are we when not being defined
Labeled
Forced

Told
Who, and how to be.

The cages around our sanity are cracking open.
The draft chills my bones.

My bravery
My courage
Shrink behind my conditioning.

Can we
Should we
Are we ALLOWED?

To breathe free air
Eat clean food

Isn't that a privilege
Not a right.

Most have been forced
Imposed upon
Overshadowed their whole life
I was

I'm working to heal the cycle
That makes me wonder
Do I belong
If so, how long

How hard do I have to work to
Earn your love
Respect
A safe place to rest

How long must I walk against the opposition that asks
me to break against the wind?

How long must I clench my fist
My jaw
Hold in my stomach
I need to be pretty to matter
I need to stifle my voice
To stay

Isn't that the way it HAS to be to live free like me

Disruptors

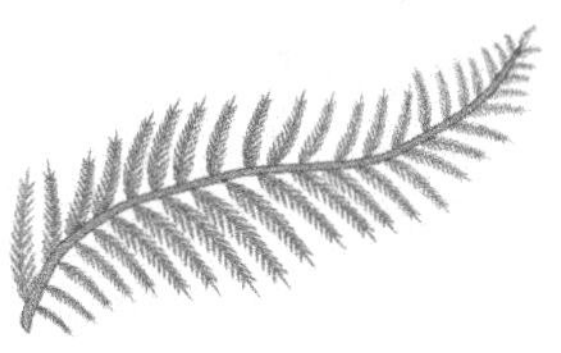

You may meet a person in your life who comes in and
turns everything upside down.
They're a disruptor.
They turn everything upside down because they know
how to care for you.
They have walked on enough pieces of glass to know
what it feels like to be cut and bleeding.
What it feels like to have something stabbing inside of
you that you can't figure out how to get out.
They may come with tweezers or tape or a soothing
salve to help while your body moves the shard out.
It isn't about romantic partnerships or planning a future
with one another.
They are here because your soul put out a signal that
said: "I want to love myself."
I need someone that can guide me back inside when
I'm most vulnerable without judging, shaming, or
criticizing me.
I need to be guided by someone who has walked this
treacherous path, who knows how to hold it
with me.
The disruptor didn't come to make things harder, even
though it might hurt to allow them to love you.
Having never been loved this way before.
Do not push them away.

Rip open your skin and let them come all the way in,
and through you.
They're expanding you beyond a conditioned love.
They're not here to do you harm.
They're here to help put things into a new
arrangement.
They are adding nuance to your life mosaic.
It will seldom look the way you imagined.
Feel the way you think it should.
This is not a thinking process.
This is divine intervention.
Helping your evolution.
The hard outer shell has to crack for everything inside
to be freed.
To know love is to touch the places you fear to be
touched.
Let the other witness these caverns inside your chest
and psyche.
Listen when they say, "It's ok to be you."
There is no insistence on you being anything different.
I am here with you.

Don't Judge

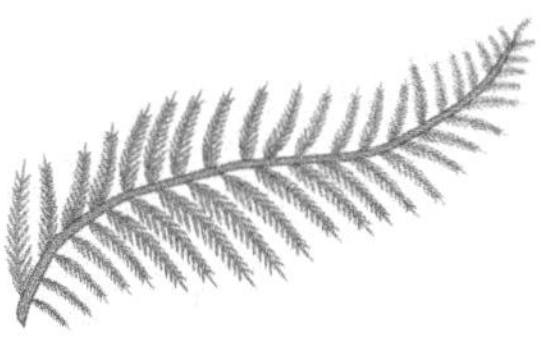

Please don't judge me by the chapter you've walked in on.

If you see a strong woman, using her voice, standing in her worth.
You missed the chapter when I was weakened and afraid.

If you see a woman who gets her writings published.
You missed the chapter when I would hide my thoughts and only keep them in my journal.

If you see a woman who speaks about her journey and healing.
You missed the chapter when I was addicted to nicotine, alcohol, and people.

If you see a mother who is proud of her children and feels connected to them.
You missed the chapter when I doubted myself every day and questioned why they chose me to be their guide.

If you see a "new agey" woman of Faith.

You missed the chapter when I felt abandoned by the Universe.

If you see someone who creates art by seeing beauty in most things.
You missed the chapter when I lived in my shadows, speaking, looking and acting from a dark place, a disconnected place.

If you see someone who is happy.
You are coming to my present chapter. It's not luck. It's the purposeful use of my thoughts, actions, and intentions.

Please don't judge me by the chapter you've walked in on.

It has taken many chapters for me to arrive here.

Dreams become Nightmares

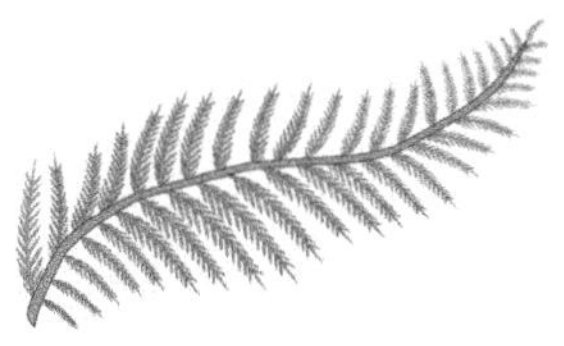

Dreams become nightmares

I know I am not alone
You know the feeling
When the place you call home
It becomes a fragmented bone
Rough edges
Gnawed
Chewed
The marrow seeps
Your heart weeps

Wondering
When did the fracture
Become a break

The heartache
The memories
The dreams that become
Nightmare

The marrow seeps

It's not to be lapped
Patched or

Brigid Hopkins

Repaired

The break
Needs to be reset
Time to mend
Regain its strength
From end to end

In this time, the marrow dries
The bone hardens
Winds shine the bones
Sealing within a new garden

Duality

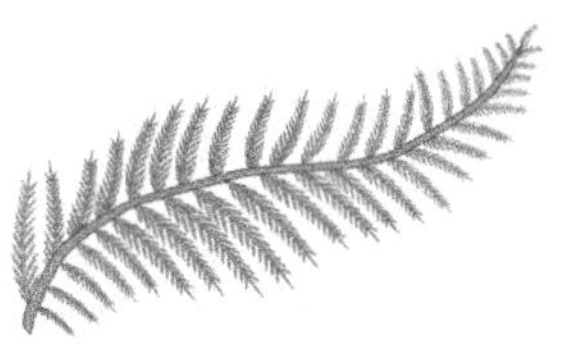

I'm ancient and juvenile
I'm brave and a scaredy-cat
I'm passionate and lazy
I'm magic and practical
I'm a dreamer and logical
I'm confident and timid
I'm intriguing and an open book
I'm wise and ignorant
I'm creative and boring
I'm funny and laugh at my jokes
(Bcz no one finds them funny)
I'm adventurous and tedious
I'm spiritual, and I curse
I'm playful and serious
I'm gregarious and shy

As you can see, it's not cut and dry. These are examples of duality. In between these states are many nuances that make, me.

One is constantly evolving and broadening.

I'm celebrating my duality more and having less interest in flaws, as much as a spectrum.

Brigid Hopkins

What may seem a flaw leads to my sublimity.

Empowerment

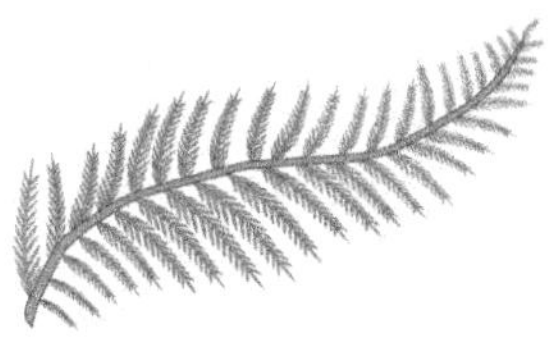

Empowerment isn't a game to be won
A conquest to strive for
Its a way of life
One that may never see mastery
But allowance
In one's blossoming
Into a fuller version of themselves

Empowerment isn't a strategy.
A task to check off the box
Its a way of life
One that requires humility
Consistency
Exploration

What looks like empowerment for me
It May not appear the same way or
Work for you

Empowerment isn't about comparison.
Follow the leader
Nor a template to
Be mapped and carved for the next
It is a unique journey for each person

One that takes them to their limit
And asks
Where to next
Will you stay here
Or go there
Where will you place your fear

To stay can be equally uncomfortable.
As taking the step
Empowerment isn't a game
A strategy
Or a task
It is a way of life
That asks
Where will you place your fear

Eros

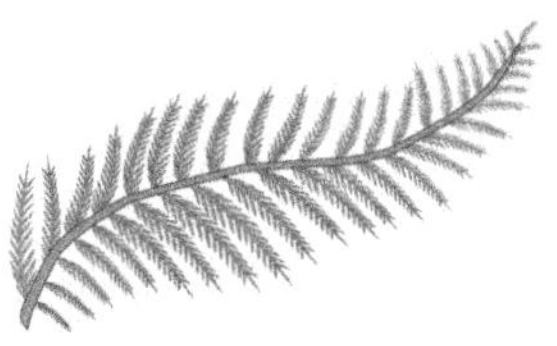

Sensuality has been on my mind. Curious to experiment with ways to nurture the essence of Eros without people.

I have a new morning practice where I wander and follow what allures me.

I spent time looking at puddles from varying angles. Watching a gaggle of geese tend to their fuzzy babies, sang to the swift current in a nearby river.

I've also taken pleasure in removing garbage from the forest.

These experiences tapped into a new channel of pleasure energy that I didn't know was possible!

It's been deeply nourishing, pleasurable, and healing.

I've no conclusion, only a growing fascination with what my body is attracted to touching.

Appreciating that attraction isn't always about another human being.

There's so much beauty, sensuality, and eroticism that stimulates our senses daily.

It's a sensual world

Everywhere

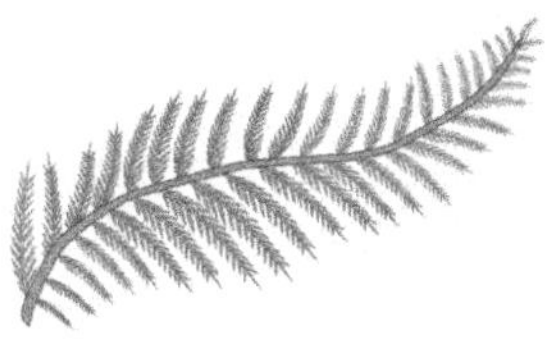

Love is trying to get your attention
In a breeze
A song
A flower
Warm sun
Rustling leaves
A hummingbird
Unexpected phone call/text
Let the love that you are
Make its way all the way inside of you
Until you're so sure of the relationship
You gift it back out

Evolving

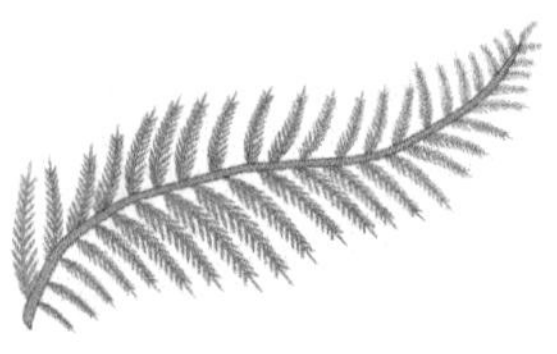

Who am I?
A year ago I would have introduced myself as Brigid the Reiki practitioner, or The epiphany midwife, his wife, or their mother.
Those fill a social curiosity of how am I productive, or successful.
Not who I am.
So, Who am I?
I'm defining that for myself a little more each day. This is what I have so far.
I am a heart, that lives in a fluffy body. I walk around each day trying to make sense of the streams of emotions, thoughts, and feelings that flow through me.
I am a human that has a loving devotion to a source called by many names. I call her Beloved.
I am a seeker with endless curiosity of all the why's in life.
I am a hugger, cuddler, lover and giver and receiver.
I am here.
I am honoring this experience.
I am, me.

Falling

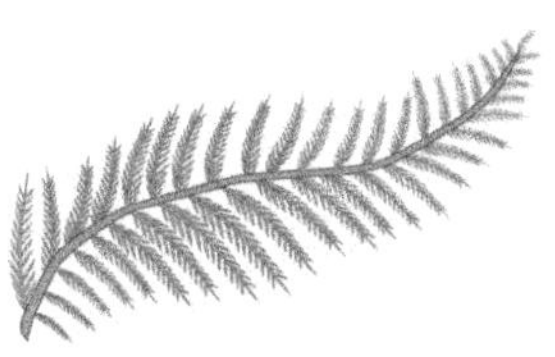

I am falling into me, the me that I have worked hard
to be.
It hasn't happened overnight, or by surprise, it's been a
thousand steps.

I say falling because it reminds me of a childhood game
I once played.
It was a trust exercise.
You picked a buddy, and they would stretch their arms
out behind you. The goal was to trust they would
catch you and just let yourself fall back.

It sounds simple.
It was a challenging game to buy into, in that phase of
my life.
My muscle for trusting others or myself was unde-
veloped.

I feel this exercise on a grander scale.
My partner is the Universe this time, and I am in mid-
fall.
Everything that has happened in my life to this
moment was to help me build my trust.

I know that I am well guided and supported by my family, friends, and the Universe.

What I am falling away from is the illusion of who I am.

As I look at my qualities, they held me a sense of safety while helping me grow into an adult. This next phase accepts responsibility for what this adult Brigid desires.

I adapted many strategies that served my qualities in my younger years. Now I am ready to embrace my spiritual life and welcome more balanced ways of being.

All the while, it integrates and accepts the gifts that those qualities had offered me.

My ego has been well skilled at keeping me going.

I love and appreciate my ego very much!

It always has a place with me in life, just not as the main driver.

It is time for me to step into the role and lead us both into the path that aligns with our soul's purpose.

Father's Day

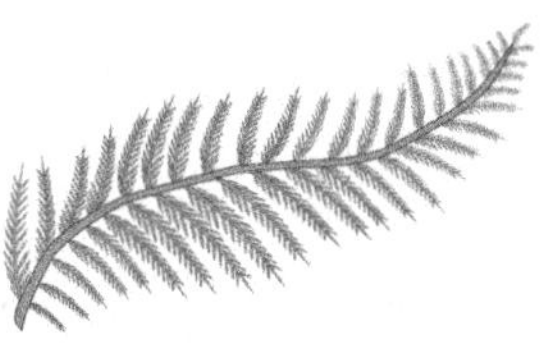

Father's day used to come with a heft of dread. I would avoid social media at all costs because the pain was too much to bear. So many happy families, children who know and celebrate the numerous lessons their Father taught them. The other children whose fathers had passed away were mourning what never came to be or the loss of greatness.

Today I made a few conscious decisions that I would like to celebrate along with everyone else. I shared my story with our children. They've heard bits and pieces, but now they are at the age to listen to my daddy's story in its entirety.

My Father was in a relationship with my mom. One thing led to another, and I was born. I'm not sure if they weren't ready to be a couple or assume the responsibilities of having a child. That part only they would know, and they both took it to their graves. I found out who my Father was the day of my Mother's funeral. To that point. I had a man's name on my birth certificate that I never knew or met. I was told growing up that my daddy died in a car accident. It seemed accurate and helped me countless times when asked, "Where's your dad?"

The longing you see that never was quelled by the story of the car accident. I so desperately wanted to know the other half of my DNA. Curious about the simplest things; his smile, his walk, the sound of his voice, his hobbies, what his life was like growing up.

The gift that came from finding out who my dad was is that I can now visit him at the cemetery every year. Something that has come to bring me a lot of peace. However, his tombstone reads Beloved Son and Brother, which pangs a bit. I was his secret just as he had been mine. He died at 45, just four months after my wedding day. My mother walked me down the aisle, and I secretly pretended that my Father was right alongside us. I pretend that a lot.

As we wound down discussing the story, I shared that I remember seeing a picture of John when I was young and me. We were at an amusement park here in Ohio, and I was holding his hand. When I found out who my dad was, it all made sense. Why have I held onto that image so firmly in my mind over the years? Maybe a tiny part of me saw the similarities we shared, and I "knew" instinctively we belonged to one another. <3

Today my daughter and I drew pictures to celebrate and honor my daddy. I went from a memory of how he looked to me as a young girl. She captured what she believed he would like later in life. It was beautiful to share this with my children, inviting his memory with us.

On the way to visit him, I had forgotten to bring him flowers. I knew I had to let my disappointment go because we were too far to turn back. When we arrived at his tombstone, numerous flowers were decorating it. I smiled and thanked him for again easing my heart.

He knows me so well.

Fear to Faith

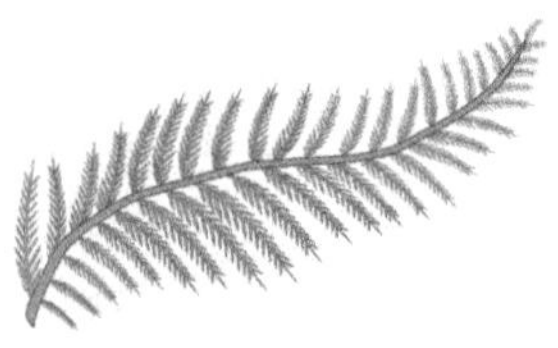

Fear shows up for me when I wish to share my truth. My default is to do what's familiar or expected, but that seldom is what I REALLY want to do.

Ten things influenced/driven by fear:

Finances ~ All of my needs would meet or exceed what I could imagine.

Intimacy ~ I wouldn't be timid or engage or attend to other people's needs first. I would put myself first and open to pleasure.

My weight ~ Caring for my body wouldn't be an afterthought or sabotage

My devotion to source ~ I can handle the higher vibrations and act of service/connection.

Living alone ~ I would dictate my values and wishes in my home.

Relationship with my children ~ I would be free of the worry that I am not a good mother or meeting their needs.

My Marriage ~ I would trust that my partner is a divine relationship and not out of need/convenience.

Driving my car ~ I would release fears of any

anxiety or worry that I will experience a panic attack again.

Growing my business ~ I would have more than enough clients to pay monthly rent and supplies. I have a valuable service!

Committing ~ I would trust my intuition, path, and the divine. I wouldn't worry that I was investing my time, energy, or money in the wrong opportunity.

Believing my worth and that I'm enough ~ It's a daily effort to affirm my worthiness. That my actions are always my best, and enough, when I open to the divine, my doubt can wash away.

3. When my strong emotions come forth, I wish to share them with another. I worry that I appear as a complainer, weak, or ineffective in my life.

1. I would experience deeper connections, self-trust, and feel free.
2. Inner peace
3. Isolation and self disconnect
4. I would feel empowered by chance to open up, honestly and sincerely. Unworried about the outcome.
5. I need to continue going at my pace and growing my connection with the divine. All of this is available to me. I will sit and offer myself to this opening!

I am feeling the expansion of this growth. The release of the armor around my heart allows more flow and energy to come into my being.

It's an adjustment, one that is welcome!

I am safe, loved, and guided.

Feeder Fish

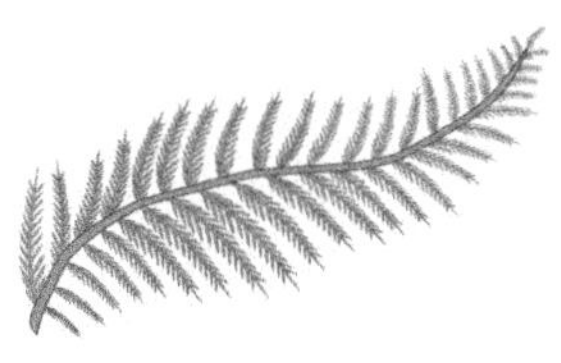

It's easy to lurk behind giving
Hide my pain
Hide my sorrow
All in the name of being "good."
Doing "good"
Planting my gardens have been a distraction
Saying yes to too many projects is a distraction
One-sided relationships
All in the name of giving and doing
Now, I stop
Put on the brakes
I begin to dive into the muddy waters of why?
Why am I afraid to say no?
Why am I afraid to feel?
Why am I afraid, to be honest?
Saying no is good
Boundaries are good
Doing what feels suitable for me, is good
I have believed the noise and judgments
Now I listen only to the tick of my heart
She knows what is best
I needn't second guess
No longer will I be the feeder fish to everyone's energy
That pond is too small for me

I will cast my sails into the unknown
Carrying me to the only place to call home
Heart

FIBERS

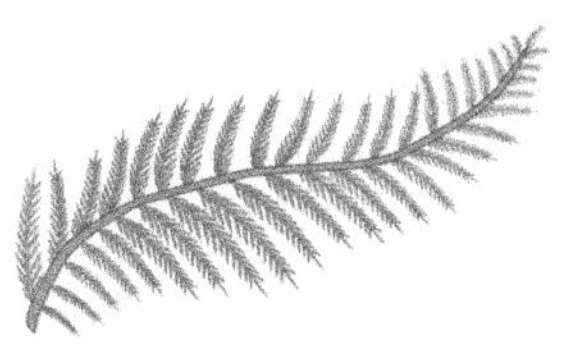

My heart is a fibrous container.
You found your way in working your way through all of the strands.
Deactivating my defenses with promises.
To be the one who wouldn't hurt this precious space.
To be the one that would listen to the deeper voices within.
Promises listen when no words are spoken.
Breathing in and breathing out with me.
In step

You did what you could.
You brought your colors.
To weave in between what was you, what was me.

Your stitches felt more like glue.
Sticky, messy, hardened, and dry.
All those hours spent wondering why I let you in.
Why did I believe you when you said all those things to my heart, not my head. You made promises that you couldn't keep.
The dirty corners of your own life are untended.
You came to me, trying to be something you couldn't be to yourself.

My tears didn't need promises from you. My heart
believed you.
We weren't looking for perfect.
We weren't looking for promises.
We were looking for sincerity.

A space to rest.
A space to be known.
A space to wander without expectation. Not a house, a
home.
The address that was once ours filled to the brim with
scars of unanswered promises.
I leave you the keys.

Taking from the space everything that belongs to me.
Dignity
Respect
Self-love

I will no longer hold someone above my propriety.
Thank you for doing your best.
It's time to listen within your chest.
Offering what is genuine and true.
There's no more prolonged pressure to be anyone
but you.

Finale'

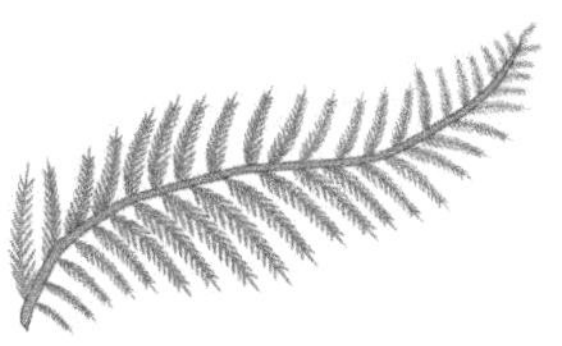

No more

No more false sense of intimacy.
No more "I'm fine."
No more smiles when I'm sad.
No more laughter when I'm gutted inside.
No more being there when I can't hold my pain.
No more doing when I'm exhausted.
No more listening when my mind is full.
No more hiding when I need help.
No more pretending my feelings are silly, misguided, or unnecessary.
No more sparing another when it cost my integrity.
No more shaming myself when I've nothing to be ashamed of.
No more lying to myself when I know what I want.
No more stifling my voice when it's my portal of courage.
No more avoiding my inner work, when it's the only way through.
No more I can handle it when I'm scared.
No more believing another's opinion of me when I know who I am.
No more.
No more.

All I can do to be true is say this, no more hiding who I am from you.

Forgiveness

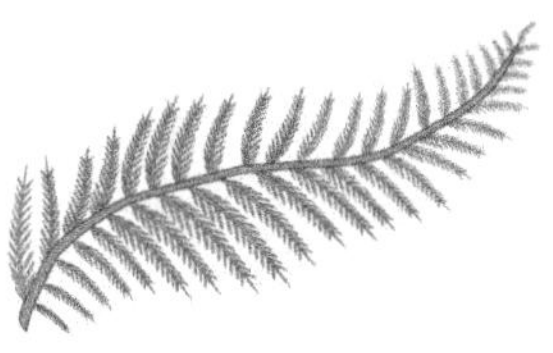

Today I

Forgive me
Forgive my neglect
Forgive my past
Forgive my ignorance
Forgive my mistakes
Forgive my darkness
Forgive my lack of boundaries
Forgive my righteousness
Forgive that I've ignored my Divinity

Fragments

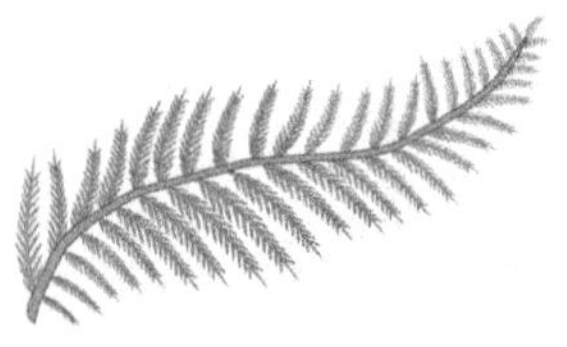

Under every rock, an expectation
Wedged in the crevices, unfulfilled dreams
In the corners dusty remnants of memories

These imperceptible fragments of
Moments
Thoughts
Plans
Hopes
Impressions
Floating
Waiting
For a moment

When I'll come back to claim them
So much of who I aspired to be
Lives in the jagged remains
Of life's mosaic

Insanity to piece together what will never be
Standing on the four corners
Ancestral, past, present, potentiality

Where can I begin
Who can I befriend

Relieved of being my enemy
Deceiving my present
Marred reality

My footbeds singed
Running against the wind

I turn to the luminous sun
Warm me in its ease
Releasing wants masked
As needs

This breath
Is for me
I fill
Empty
Through eternity

Gifts

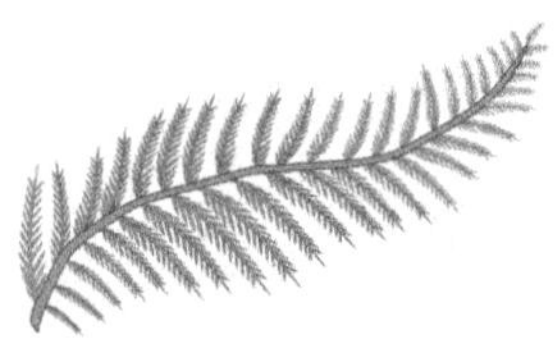

Every time we doubt our magic
We dilute it

Every time we hide our ability
We dilute it

Every time we deny our voice
We stifle it

Every time we say we don't know
We deny the truth

Every time we hide our talent
We dilute it

Each person has a unique soul signature with specific challenges to face, learn, and give from.

As the receiver, we need to be mindful of judging another person.

Our job as the receiver is to be present with what is.
Listen
Observe
Feel

See
Know

If what is offered is good for us, now.
It may not be the right time, but that doesn't make it wrong.

Some things need time to curate in our psyche before we can allow.

Know that most of us here have big magic and we are afraid to use it because we've been judged for it our whole lives!

We want a better world too.

The delivery of our magic takes skill.
It takes feedback
It takes receptivity
It takes cooperation
It takes courage from both sides.

It is time to stop hiding our magic
The world needs our consciousness
To mend
To grow
To birth
A new world

Good Hands

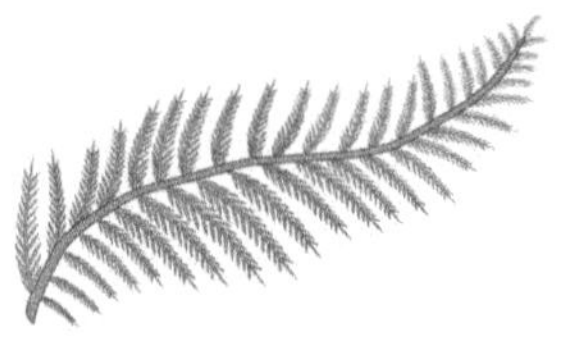

We are in good hands.

When the World news feels dismal
look within your community
Who are you?
What can you do?

When the environmental issues overwhelm you,
Look within your heart.
Who are you?
What can you do?

When the political division causes you to quake in
anger,
look for the one who needs your help.
Who are you?
What can you do?

If you say, who me?
I am no one.
There's nothing to be done.
I say look to the sky.
Feel the Earth
Taste the water
Breathe

These are you.
You are as big as the sky
Deep as the ocean
Old as the soil

There is nothing you CAN not do.
Please remember you are here because all the odds of creation were in your favor.

I ask you again.
Who are you?
What can you do?

Grief

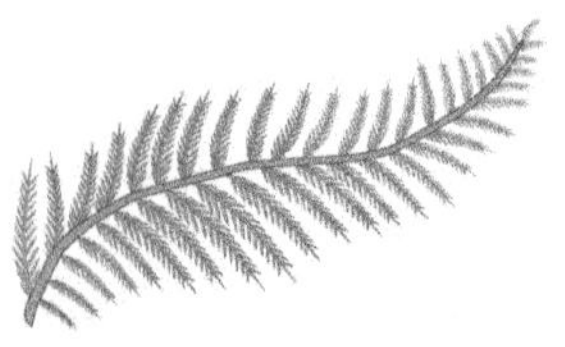

I've been processing grief.

Many different shapes and textures of grief are moving through me, some my own, some not.

Grief is something I used to turn away from, fearing it would consume me. Through many paths and cycles of grieving, I've learned it never leaves; it accompanies me.

Now it's with me as a companion. Some days it needs more of my attention than others.
I took to the woods to move my body and give this grief more space to flow. I'm so grateful for feelings, emotions, and evolving ways to be with what is.

Nature soothes.

Handled

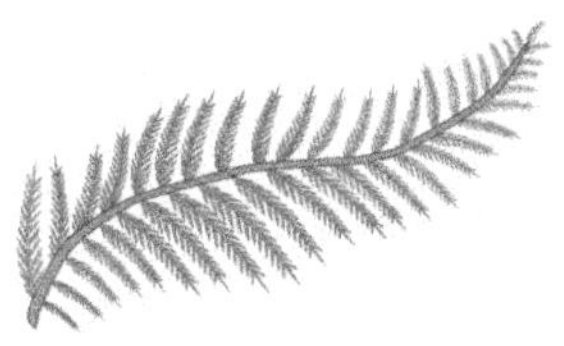

Since birth, I have been handled
Placed
Told
When to rest, eat, be
Even as an adult, I follow the map
The one laid by my upbringing
I have played and experimented
But the deeply worn ruts call me back
Back to my conditioning

I now permit myself to be
Be with darkness
Purposefully retreat to
Slowed to imperceptible breath

I need this more than I've given credit to
Caving is a means of restoration for my beingness
I feel most myself after resting in the dark

I no longer ignore the primal call for this need
To be tended
The noise of this world drives me to my borders
I pace myself into my stillness

Remembering the sacredness of reconnection

Of the walled allegory
I decorate the rolling structures not with force
Or friction
Simple noticing

Where do I place the next color
Texture
Imprint
Which part of my cavern is asking
For gentle attention

I lay here feeling into
An echoed response
Then, only then, do I add
A new decor
To my heartened cosmology

Heart

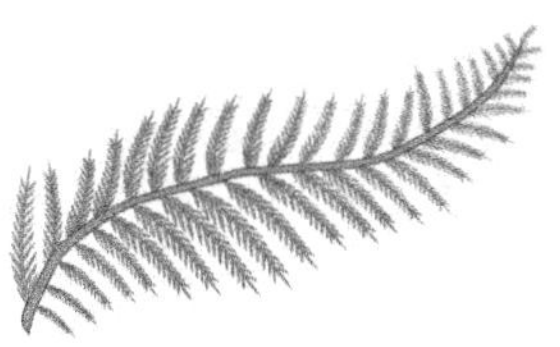

Art
Ear
Tear
Hear

There is no Fear in Heart.

Hiding

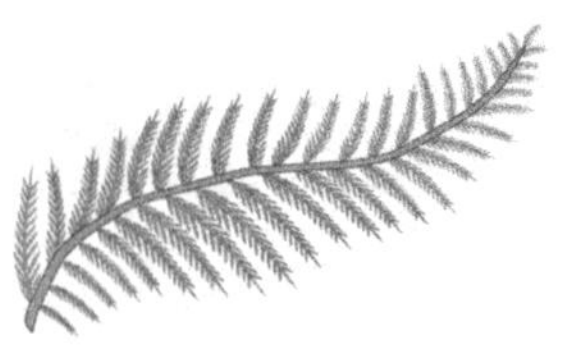

A piece of my inner world that most may not know is that I live most of my life afraid.

Afraid to be known
Afraid to be heard
Afraid to be seen
Afraid no one would like me
Afraid I didn't matter
Afraid of being too much
Afraid I'm imposing
Afraid I'm a fraud
Afraid I'm not good enough
Afraid I will fail
Afraid to try
Afraid to stop

These beliefs formed many years ago in my psyche as coping mechanisms that I created as a measure to keep myself safe, secure, and at a distance. I didn't want people to be too close to me or know too much of me because it wasn't safe. When anyone came close to my perimeter, I felt threatened.

These coping mechanisms didn't die off. They rooted deeper and drove harder my tendencies to push off, run away or avoid anything that would put me in direct contact with being vulnerable—not knowing which is worse, being exposed or feeling threatened. I began testing the waters, making new choices, and trying different ways of slowly poking my head out, sharing my voice, being visible in the world.

Through my work, I learned these places of fear and hiding as stemming from my Inner child. I call her my Feral child. She would cower and hiss at the sight of me, too untrusting of my connection attempts. Over time I am getting to know her more and more and beginning to understand her nature, wounding, and needs. It's a slow, tedious process, as everything she holds comes from my entire lifetime. She was the one protecting me during abuse. She was the one keeping me safe.

My inner child rose through a recent experience in my women's circle. However, I was not wholly conscious of this at the time. What happened was my actions of speaking up for myself, and letting be known what didn't feel good to me, were supporting her integration. She finally trusted me enough to come forward with her needs and see that I would meet them. My sisters held me tightly and loved me through the integration. My feral child grew and blossomed into a slightly older form of herself. Less wild, wily,, and dirty. She was well-kempt, sparkly, and happy.

My Feral child didn't only keep away threats; she also

blocked love, closeness, and connection. Relationships of love were equally as threatening to her. Believing that I'm unlovable made it impossible for anyone to show me their love, tell me of their love, or give me love.

It bounced off of my armoring. There was nowhere for it to come in. The integration allowed my armoring to fall and cracks of light to stream through.

The light that strewn out also left room for the love to come in. Those who love me can step closer and not thwart their efforts by my fears.

Holding Finite

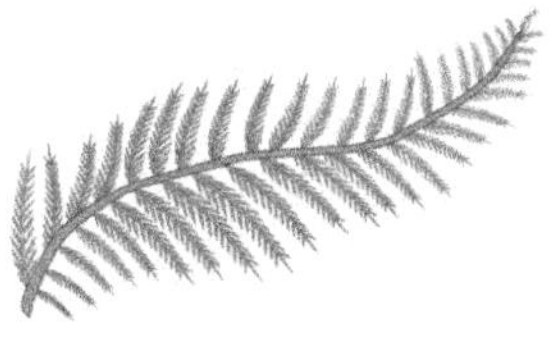

Holding the finite
Guides me through

The yesterday's that mattered to an idea that I can no longer recall.

Tiredness from bending over myself to please and be something I never could be.

Stroking the skin and veins of what remains to borrowed Earth on two feet.

Crows' feet complement the glimmer streaks of white painting my crown.

Age
Time
Pretense
Matter very little
When the season comes to a close

Drinking in the sun
Swinging on the breeze
Touching roots
Nestled with relations

Slowly curling, sinking in
For a long Winter's sleep.

How do I know?

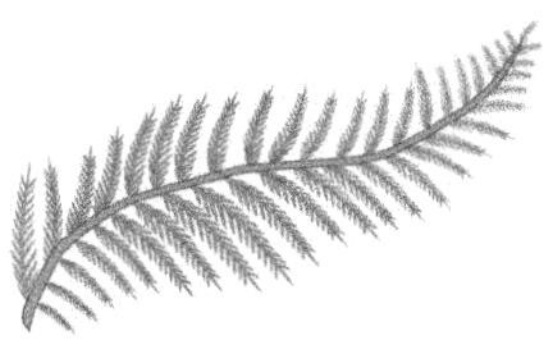

How do I know when I am healed
How do I know when my mask has fallen away
How do I know when I mean what I say

Who is animating this body
Who is looking from behind the brown eyes
Who is the voice that speaks my name

How do I come to know these parts of me
When I have am the product of my conditioning

I look in the mirror, and it takes me five minutes to
move past
All of the names
Facades
Lost expectations
Of my derivation

How do I know when I am healed
How do I know when I am real
How do I know what I feel

When I am the product of my conditioning

How many goals are of my creation

Brigid Hopkins

How many accomplishments renew my legacy
How many times do I need to prove myself to the void?

It never matters more to them than I believed
How do I come to know the genuine parts of me

How do I know that what I see is of me
How do I know when I am awake within the dream
Of my perceived reality
Or this another condition of my conditioning

Hurried

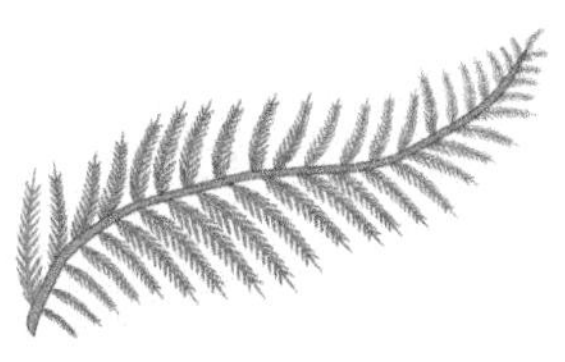

Anything hurried is a missed encounter
Food shoveled in
Racing to meet a friend
Quickies with your beloved
Alarms chiming throughout the day

There has to be more to life than urgency

Haste
Waste
Longing

Long strokes
Deep conversations
Steeping tea
Reminiscing
Fantasizing

Dropping goals
Agendas
Roles
History

Gives way to
Playful encounters

With beavers
Otters
Along the river banks

Praying
Giving thanks
To the great mystery

We are birthed for more
Than hurry
Worry
Strife

We came to experience
Life
In its fullness
Delights
Making friends along The way
Greeting the sun

Touching the stars
In our fantasy
Dreaming
Beaming
Exploring
Territory
That is free
Wild
Lush

She knows she is safe
In the great escape
From humanity

I Believe in God

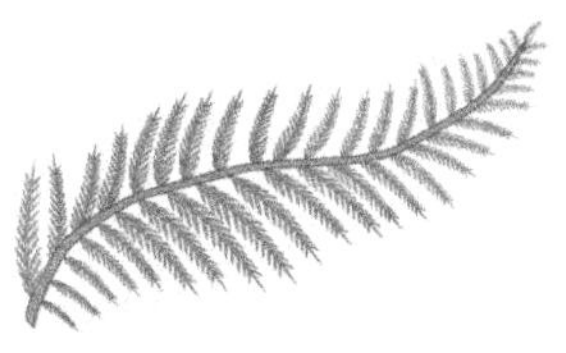

I believe in God
An energy that is the creator of all things
Big and small
I do not believe in a big man in the sky
Holding a staff of judgment
Waiting to strike me down when I have sinned
I believe in mistakes
I believe in low moments
I believe that my God
Allows me to be Brigid
A human who came for an experience
Not judgment
To lead a life of winding missteps
Allowing me to fail
Fall
Climb
Each time I felt weary
God was the fingertip on my heart
Reminding me, I am here
I am breathing
Try again
All of the shame
Guilt
Regret I hold in my being
It isn't because I let God down

I let myself down
The self that has held standards dictated by society
A society I do not align with
God has always allowed me
To be sovereign
Not a drone
Letting my inner knowing lead me home
The same home God lives in
The place I keep sacred
Expanding
Well insulated
Beginning with H
Beats
Ends with T

I Don't Know

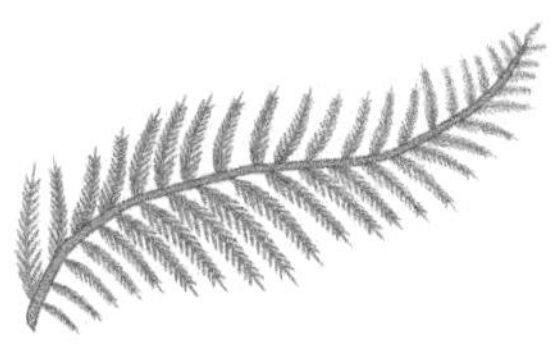

You say you don't know
But you do
You pretend you don't know
But you do
You believe you don't know
But you do
The difficulty is claiming your knowing
Owning what you know at the moment
Making what is true for you known and
Accepting the outcome

Our minds will convince us of just about anything to keep us where we are. It's not that our mind doesn't like us. Our mind is trying to keep us safe from any perceived threat. Being known is scary. Being responsible is scary. Standing in the flames of your fire is terrifying.

Sticking with, I don't know.
Dishonors all that you are.
All that you are capable of achieving.
It keeps you in a tiny place.
You are more significant than you can comprehend.

When that voice creeps in and begins to say, "I don't
know."
With the next breath, ask;

What are you afraid to say?
What are you afraid to know?
What are you afraid to see?
What are you afraid to claim?
Are you willing to be curious?
Are you willing to investigate?

And if you still don't know.

Leave SPACE to find out.

I don't know is the beginning, not an end.

I am a burden

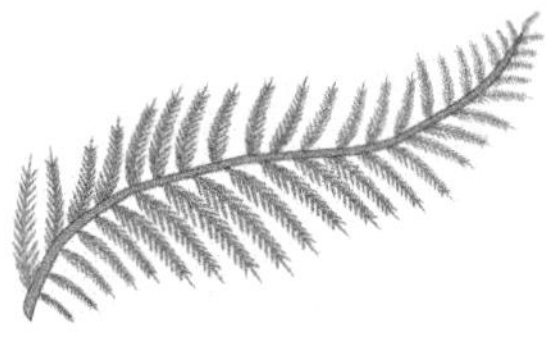

Are you feeling like a fish out of water?

I wonder this as I am being shot out of the water and come onto land.

How can I breathe when the very thing I've depended on is no longer available? This can be a belief, strategy, relationship, coping mechanism, etc.....

It's the shadow belief of "I'm a burden."

Where can I source oxygen?
When not using the preferred or usual method that kept me submerged?

Strategy - "I've got it. I don't need help. I'm fiercely independent."

Where can I find the ground again?

Who am I when my darkest matter is present?
In what ways do I judge myself for the less than desirable behaviors?
What ways do I hide?

The CRAB has sharp claws for defense. It can have a snappy disposition. But that isn't who the crab is; it is what it does to protect that very vulnerable underbelly. Its only means of staying alive and safe are to charge towards the threat.

This New Moon, we are in the dark. The underbelly of the self. The shadow side may be holding powers and strengths we aren't conscious of.

So I dare to ask....

Am I interested in becoming aware?

Am I willing to look into the dark?

Am I ready to face the places and spaces that scare me?

Who am I when vulnerable?

Where does my crabby nature live?

Am I willing to stop putting this self in the closet?

Am I willing to let these powers be known?

Am I ready to unite with more of my wholeness?

All of us carry archetypal energies that have been under persecution from the mainstream. Think of the liar, thief, martyr, victim, vampire, slut. It does no one well to deny these parts of self. They are thirsting to be accepted. To be recognized. To be FREED.

The energies I keep sensing are asking these hard questions because liberation is asking to be known....

Do I have the courage to be my liberator?

To accept the places inside of me that are monstrous? If I free them, what then? Won't I be hurting others? The destruction I fear of placing outside of myself is already happening inside.

How is it helping the world keep suppressing the things that scare me? Self-acceptance doesn't have to be a public event. But rather to stand in the darkness with compassionate witnessing and openness to its power and fury. Hold these hurting places and say, there, there I'm here. I won't abandon you or judge you anymore.

I am here.

That type of action and acceptance isn't causing pain to another. It is helping the hurt.

It is a request for more love, not less. To accept the ignored, dismissed, and denied parts of my being. No longer stand on the head of "I'm a burden" and deny that part of myself the dignity of being known.

If I come to you

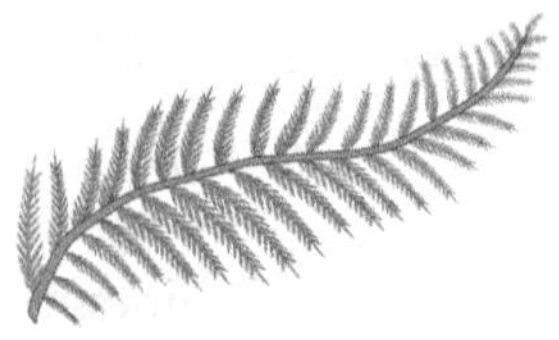

If I come to you
Will you receive me

If I chatter at you
Will you receive me

If I come in flames
Will you receive me

If I come as a flurry
Will you receive me

If I come crawling
Will you receive me

If I am destitute
Will you receive me

If I am delusional
Will you receive me

If I am fanatical
Will you receive me

A small calm voice whispers back. I already have. It is

you who doesn't receive my acceptance, my love, my steadfast devotion.

You are not yet willing to receive me.
I always believe in you.

I lay longer in this place, waiting for my next wave to take me deeper into self-acceptance. It is here I wait to receive all of me.

Infinity

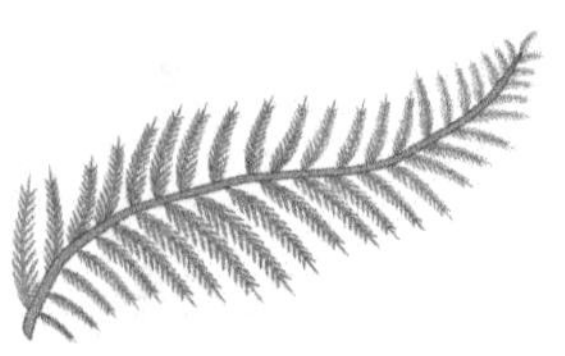

Infinity
Impermanence
Love
Intimacy
Nature
Delicate
Strength
Where do I fit in the pool of timelessness
Only my heart knows for sure

Inner Child

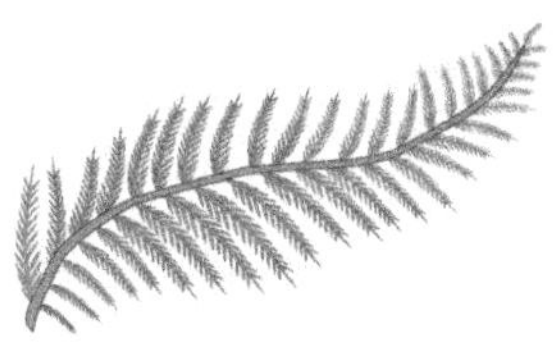

In the quiet of the morning, she spoke
I listened
When is the war between us and the world
Going to end?
When will it stop being us vs. them?
You can lay down your sword.
Knowing that all you have abhorred
Is not outside of you

Each difficult interaction
It was a moment of introspection
To see your reflection of suffering
In the eyes of the other
They were there to help you steer
Back inside of you

Bringing you closer to me

The tired, scared child that rests deep inside of you
You've tucked me away, trying to protect me

Set me free

Let me be the guide
I no longer want to hide

I trust you
Do you trust me?

The things that you hate
Are holes inside of you

The things that scare you
Are memories tucked inside of you.

The things that you envy
Are untapped wells of your divinity.

The time is now that you turn to face
The beauty and grace of all that you are.

There is pain
There is trauma
There is uncertainty
There is doubt

Do not let these things shroud
The brilliance of your offering.

They are reminders and guides of the depths
That rest inside of your becoming

Experience and knowledge
Reminders of how it felt
That you chiseled a new route
And came through the other side

It is ok to have history
It is ok to have shadows

It is ok to have grit
It is ok to have failures
It is ok to have regret
It is ok to have shame

None of these things define who you are to me
You are the one that carries us both
Stoking flames and fires
Letting our desires breathe and burn
Churning the oil that once kept you stagnant
Into glowing embers

I trust you
I believe in you
I ask again
Set me free

Let us merge and rise
To the dawning of our unity.

It had to be you

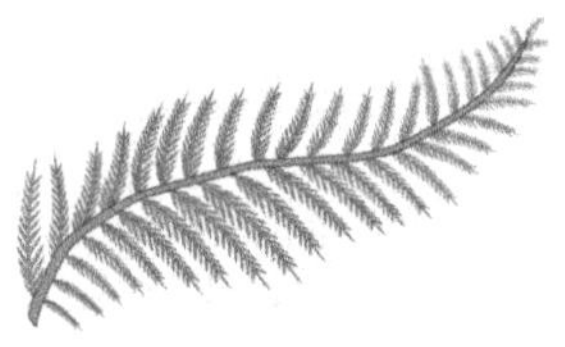

It had to be you
To reach inside
Of my darkness
Unafraid of the shadows
I was living in
I had no idea how far
I traveled
Until you found me there
I, too afraid of your familiarity
With the dark
I am grateful
Thankful
Eased
If you hadn't experienced
The depths
You wouldn't have known the
Way
Thank you for finding me
For showing me
That no matter how far
One travels
They're loved
They're seen
They're worthy of
Resurrection

Redemption
All of the time, I worried about you
You were preparing to save me
The irony
Daughter
Thank you for bringing
Back to the light

Joy

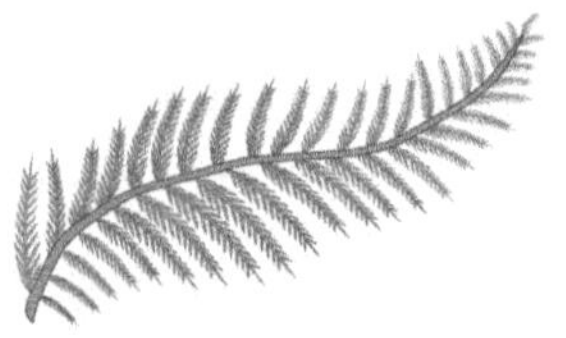

You arrived
In my depths of despair
Holding hands with grief
You stood fair

I looked over her casket
Remembering the words
That never left my lips.

Tears streaming
You comfort me
Remember the good times

Breathe easy
This ending
Is an opening

To a tomorrow you can't yet see

The tears kept coming,
Heart aching

You reminded me that history,
Does not dictate the present
Here

And
Now
You are a guest in the mess
Of this transition

As grief grips me
You soothe me
As regret burns me
You cool me

Our relationship
Began there
An early introduction
To a long evolution
Of welcoming
Joy

Letting Love In

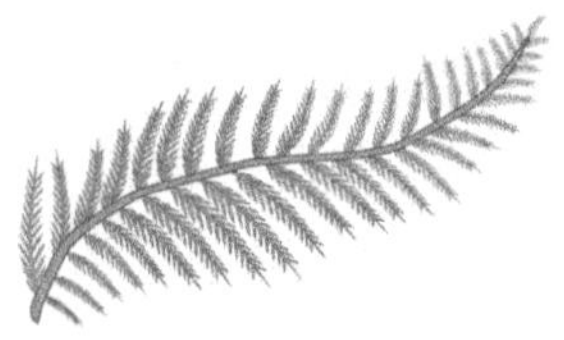

I know sorrow
I know misery
I know suffering
I know self-torment
I know abuse
I know isolation
I know terror

I still carry trauma
I still work at healing
I still see my wounds
I still act in ways I regret
I still scream when no one is looking
I still face the roughest edges of my psyche
I still ditch being responsible here and there

What is different

I pray
I write
I cry
I speak
I meditate
I serve
I standstill

I ask for help
I share with others
I let it all the way down

I stop believing my lies
I stop believing nothing will change
I stop believing I have no authority
I stop believing there's no hope
I stop believing that I am unlovable
I stop believing that I am not enough
I stop believing that I won't succeed
I stop believing the stories that rutted me to
 the past

I'm ready to let love in
I'm ready to let love cleanse me
I'm ready to let love renew me
I'm ready to let love hold me
I'm ready to let love mend me
I'm ready to let love break the old binds
I'm ready to let love illuminate my hollows
I'm ready to let love fill me

Letting love in
Trying what love can do
It is an act of Faith
Surrender
Trust

Giving myself to something I cringe at over and over
 again.
Giving myself to something that I've conditioned
 myself against

Giving myself to something that I may never master in this lifetime
Giving myself the chance to be loved and NOT run away from it
Giving myself the opportunity to know who I am when I am touching love

Self-love offers this;
Stop harboring ill-feelings because of things you didn't know at the time!
Stop harboring ill feelings towards yourself because you didn't know another way to manage your reaction.
Stop holding yourself back from being in alignment because it's scary.
Stop holding yourself back from what you most desire because of who you have been in the past.

These stories only carry the weight you lend them. If you take away the fuse, they don't ignite!

Turn towards your self-love and stop being your own worst friend.

Let love in
Let love lead
Let love guide
Let love convince you
Let love shoulder your worry
Let love move you forward
Let love be your new anchor

Letting People Down

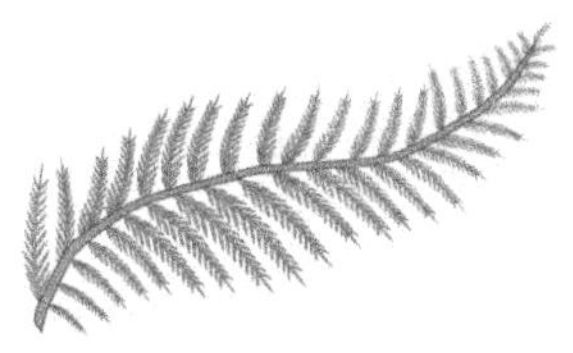

I've let people down
I didn't show up when I said I would
I raised my voice more than I needed to
I promised to return a call -- I never did
Outstanding agreements--went unmet
I ditched numerous projects that began with high
hopes--left with smoldering disappointment.
I have tried and failed countless times.

If I let you down
Know that I let myself down first
It was never intentional
It was unavoidable
As I was hiding from myself
Hiding from you
Blinded by my blind spots
I chose the more challenging path
The one that led to disappointment
Regrets
Embarrassment

There were lessons for both of us
I can't give what I don't have
Learned to be responsible for my energy
Time

And commitments
Do not make promises I can't keep
Do not expect to give when I am struggling, hiding, or
in denial
Know that I am harder on myself than you would
imagine
Trust that I am learning the lesson even when I do it
again
Sometimes I have to fall twice to pick myself up all
the way

I've let people down.
AND
I've shown people how to get back up
To make the call, even if its years later
Ask for forgiveness
Let go of shame
Be kinder to oneself
Live with integrity
Give back projections
Own my shadows
Mistakes are inevitable; it's how we grow
I've let people down
More importantly, how to get back up again.

Lift

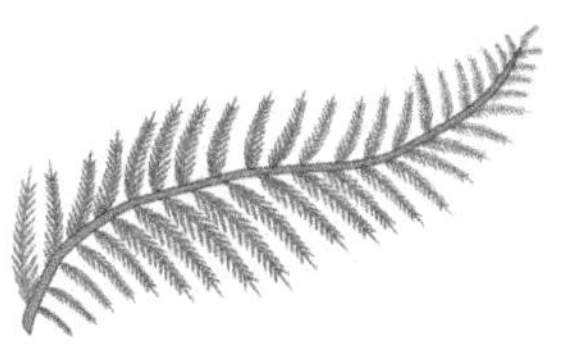

It is humanity's responsibility to lift one another, see the good, be the good and honor the dark.
When someone is struggling, do not add.
Lift
When someone is lost, do not ignore them.
Lift
When someone is scared, do not add.
Lift
When someone forgets they matter, remind.
Lift
Our life is about wholeness.
We are having experiences.
We aren't bred to do this alone.
We are wired for connection and communing.
L-love
I- intentionally
F-fiercely
T-this moment

Making Dreams Come True

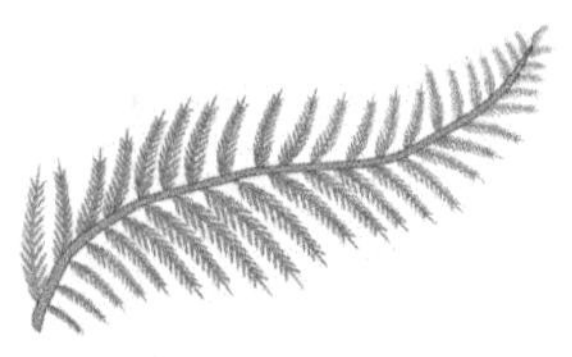

I make my dreams come true
I'm not unique
You can do this to
It takes time
Patience
More time
More patience
Humor
And good men and women like you
The ones who listen when I don't speak
Who see when I am not there
That check-in often with loving care
You do not assume or impose
Instead, you open the windows
Dust me off
Say good job
Keep going
You've got the right stuff
You've believed in me so that I could do the same
One painstaking day after day
Giving up isn't who you are they say
Take more time
More patience
Go another way
Around and around I went

In and out
Up and down
Backward.. You get the gist
Now I am here on the cliff
Jumping off to who knows where
When or why
I give my thanks as I continue to soar
With you by my side

Menopause

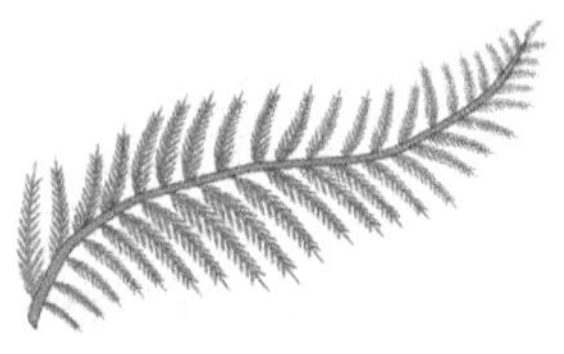

Walking myself home
To the second act
It was a terrifying thought
In my twenties
Still far away in my thirties
And ushering me forward
In my forties

As I heard the stories
The dread
Inconvenience
Aggravation
Through others experiences

I wondered how I would fare?
Would I mind having graying hair?
Would I have to relinquish my youth?
Too childish for a fifty-something

The time nears
I am gladdened by the
Approaching change

I frolic
I squawk

I roll down hills
Splash in puddles
Chase sunsets
Wake to greet the day
Speak in earnest
Leave my face naked
Hair unkempt

No longing
Or sorrow
For my younger times
To season
Along with my thicker skin

Life is a flower
I savor the sweetness of
Each hour
No complaints

Mining and Tending

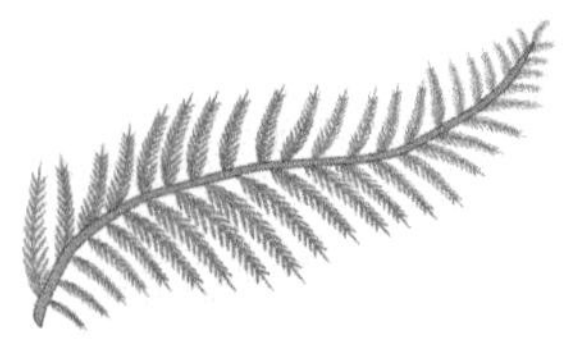

I do care what people think
Of me
Our world
Their propriety

Not from vanity
From heart

At the very start, we are looking
At another's eyes
Hands

Hearing their opinions and voice
In near and distant lands

Not from judgment
From Innocence

Children grow through
Womb
Environment
Expectations
Experimentation

Not from ignorance

From Curiosity

It's from the heart
That I wish to know
How I affect you
Impose upon you
Inspire
How we tangle and revel
In the fate of being human

Not from politeness
From sincerity

I do not fear your opinions
As my child and adult
I have grown into a frame
Of shifting identity
No longer bound
To conformity
I ask, and I care
What you think of me
For my reflection is you
And you are me
We are mirroring
Our reality

From illusion
To clarity

To say I don't care
what you think of me
Is a denial of our mutual
Existence

I do care
I do observe
Adjust
Intend
Amend
And
Trust

That you care too...

Mirror Goes Black

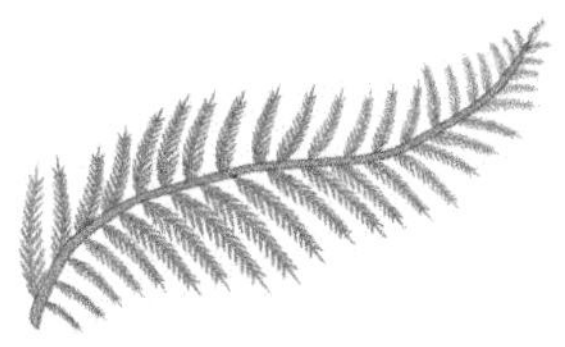

The mirror went black
Stop it!
Stop it right now!

Stop what?

Stop looking for what is wrong
Stop looking with yesterday's eyes
The eyes of your peers
Your family
Your mentors

Stop looking for what isn't there
Anything you see is either
Memory
Or
Creation

Stop looking for blemishes
Fat
Blemishes
Scars

How do you know that's what I'm doing?

I see it in your eyes
I feel it in your sigh
I know it's the way you were shown

Mirrors aren't for vanity
They're for clarity

Clarifying
Fog
Distortion
Misrepresentation
Misunderstanding

Stop looking in the mirror for what isn't there
There's nothing wrong with your appearance
Your feelings
Your emotions
Are another kind of mirror

None of them rule your domain unless you believe it to be true.

So tell me
Who are you?
This moment
How does this you walk, talk, and present themself in the world outside of you?

What do you want me to see when I look at you?

Clean up anything that doesn't reflect that.

Be good to yourself and know the mirror isn't here to hurt you.

It's here to clarify what has.

Mirrors

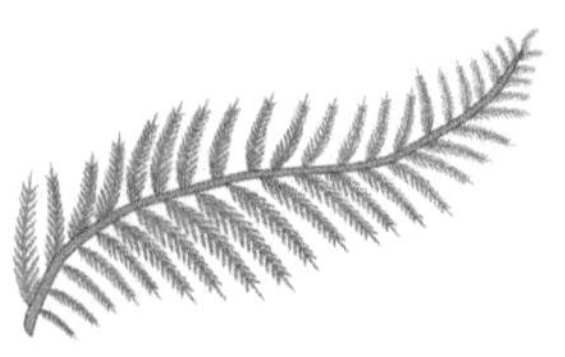

What do you see when you look in the mirror?
Mirrors are people, glass, chrome, reflections,
  water, etc.
Mirrors are everywhere in our life. What do you see
  when you allow yourself to look at what is
  reflected?

I could say my hair is wild and frizzy.
The puffiness under my eyes is growing.
My summer kissed glow is fading.
The scar in between my nose bugs me.

Or

I can look deeper into my own eyes.
See what my soul is trying to help me realize.
I am so much bigger than this costume I wear each day.
The me I see is not, the me I am
I have a wild rhythm that is growing.
It has a primal beat, not of this existence.
The countless versions of me worked to bring me to this
  now moment.

And

It is through the mirrors of people I am shedding
outdated beliefs.
I am letting go of the expectations of how I am
supposed to be, who I am supposed to be, what I
am supposed to be.
The mirrors of inanimate objects are helping me to
catch glimpses of my undomesticated self.

To get to the purer form of this primal beat.
I am allowing it to lead my heart into the unknown.
Face my fears.
Scream when I need.
Falling to my knees in humility, I do not KNOW
anything about living from this place.

If I allow the voices of this world and this race, I am too
far in, to retreat. Too curious to stop. I keep looking
in the mirrors, with my palms face up. I am willing
to receive the feral version of me.

Mother's Hand

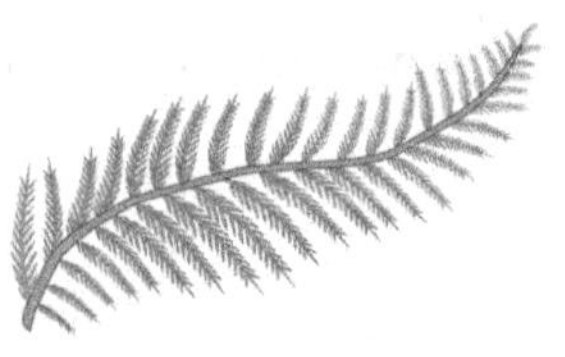

In this noisy mixed-up world
There are times I fall into stillness
Contemplation resigning my condemnation
For where our civilization is heading
There are steady hums that used to be filled with ticks
analog to digital
In the stillness, I trade in my swipes on social media
For daydreams
A time that once was, or may have never been
It comforts me the same
I imagine the countless generations of hands that have
reached into a crib
Gracing the cheeks of innocence
Sworn to protect the fragile
Raise them to fruitful adults
Repeating the cycle of home
I've held that hand
I gave it to my own
So many dreams and promises
Never quite realized
They are exhaled into the dense
Damp air this night
Weariness wears polishes the patina
I couldn't be all things
My mind lost its grip and I fell

Pressing the edges of resources
The heart is strong
My hands stronger
I pulled myself back into the now
No longer reaching for what can't be
Or promising what I decline to anticipate
I leave the imprint from all the nights
I graced their cheeks
Praying that they will remember
The hands that held them
Prayed them into form
Guarded and warmed them
Swinging to the lullabies
Giving the next generation
What they longed for
If there is still air to breathe
Water to drink
And a place to call home
The first pair of hand's
Our great Mother's
She is reaching up towards the moon
Pleading we wake from the illusion
And with great urgency
Give more than we know-how
This moment
Reprimand our misgivings
Stop looking to the past to heal the present
With eyes that hear her pleas
Reflecting back to me in the moonbeams
I watch the breath hang in the dampened air
Remember the last mother hand I held
The night she fell back into the earth

No More

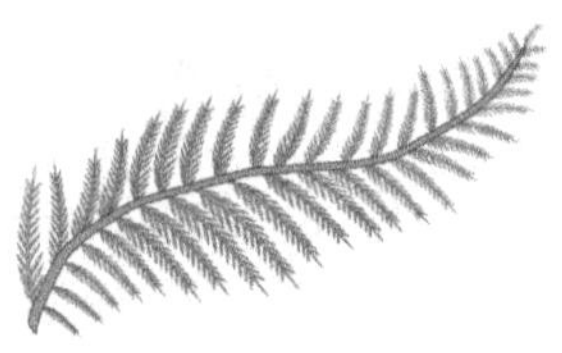

No more
No more false sense of intimacy.
No more "I'm fine."
No more smiles when I'm sad.
No more laughter when I'm gutted inside.
No more being there when I can't hold my pain.
No more doing when I'm exhausted.
No more listening when my mind is full.
No more hiding when I need help.
No more pretending my feelings are silly, misguided, or unnecessary.
No more sparing another when it cost my integrity.
No more shaming myself when I've nothing to be ashamed of.
No more lying to myself when I know what I want.
No more stifling my voice when it's my portal of courage.
No more avoiding my inner work when it's the only way through.
No more I can handle it when I'm scared.
No more believing another's opinion of me when I know who I am.
No more.
No more.

All I can do to be true is say this, no more hiding who I am from you.

No Spice

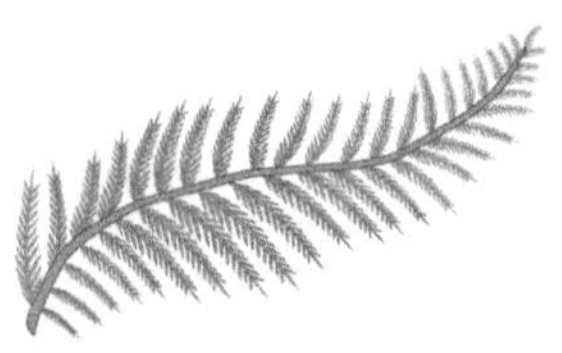

My spice cabinet is filled with herbs and seasonings to delight the senses. I feel abundant and prosperous having so many available to me. Yet, with all that avail itself to me. Why do I feel barren and incomplete?

How many jars can occupy this space until I feel there are enough?

When my problem isn't quantity, it's implementation. Clueless on how to marry the flavors. Which layer first? Do woody herbs pair well with florals? Can too much, be too much? I love flavorful food, and when I turn to my abundant shelves. I feel lost.

I don't know each herb's range or depth well. I haven't taken enough risks and chances to learn. I stay in neutral--grabbing the standby of salt and pepper!

Life is prolific and fruitful every day. How often am I missing the chance to take a risk experiment without much at stake? I mean, herbs are a no-fail way to be a bit wild and crazy!

Well, not that herb.

Ol Fashioned

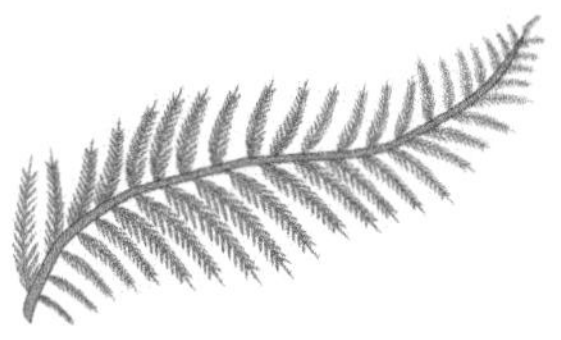

These times of
High speed
High tech
Progress
Innovation
Convenience

Leaving me wanting

Candles flicker
Absence of hums
Dings
Reminders
Quiet that can be heard for miles
Big skies
Stars along the horizon line

The insistence of connection
Because we can

Leaves me wanting

What is it like to miss someone?
Is anyone missing me?
Receive penned letters

Wondering how a faraway friend has gotten on

With the flick of a wrist, the mystery
Is explained
The sky mapped
The lights endless

This modernization
It makes me long to be old fashioned
Old worldly
Crafting for necessity
Not Etsy

It all leaves me wanting less and less of the ease of
modernity.

Please give me the grit of dirt floors
Soot stained walls
Cellars filled for winter's chill
The anticipation of a letter
A telegram
A visit
Tea on the porch
With neighbors
Pies cooling on the sill

The pace of this progress
It can leave one feeling
Ill
Inept
Too slow
Too old

Bring back the innocence
Of wonder
Exploration
Disconnect from
Google

Mend the longing
With a walkabout
No tweet
Flicker
Gram
Or book
Good ol fashioned
Time with a brook

A time to rest
For the sake of progress

Pack

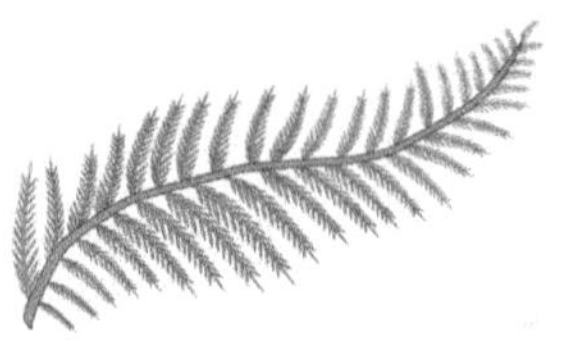

Get your pack, and don't look back.
Jim Rohn said, "You are the average of the five closest people to you."

If they're happy being a 9-5'er and you're an entrepreneur.

Do you speak the same language?
Do you lift one another to take chances?
Do they understand the fire that burns in your veins to be of service?
Do they understand when you're radio silent bcz you focus solely on the vision?

They love you.
They care.
They've always been there.
They're doing their best.

They do not see the same vista.
Different goals, needs, and agendas obstruct their view.

They smile and say they get it.
They offer advice to keep you grounded.
Help you to be more reasonable.

Another edge in the growth scale.

Your tribe will change.
You may even be lonely at times.
Wonder how did this happen?

You are making room for your pack.
The ones that will run through the darkest night, to be in position for the sunrise over the mountains.
The ones that hear your absurd ideas and up the absurdity to possible.
The ones who do not let you fall into doubt and fear, are walking alongside you, cheering you on, bcz they have felt defeat.
They have felt the call.
They were waiting for You!

Embrace your pack, and don't look back.
< wolf howl >

Pedigree

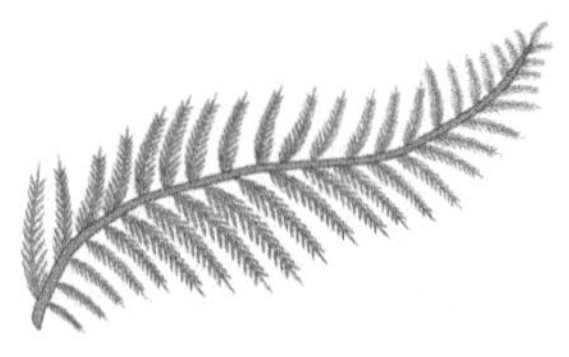

I am not a dog
I am not a horse
I am not a trophy
I am not an object

You can't tame me
You can't muzzle me
You can't delouse me
You can't stable me
You can't neuter me
You can't clip my wings

It doesn't mean they didn't try
But the beauty of a wild spirit
They will always find a way to fly

There isn't a cage
Domicile
Reckoning
Reward
Wise enough to cage this wild soul

For if you succeed
Euthanize me

It's the only decent thing to do
To earmark one's pedigree

Perfectly You

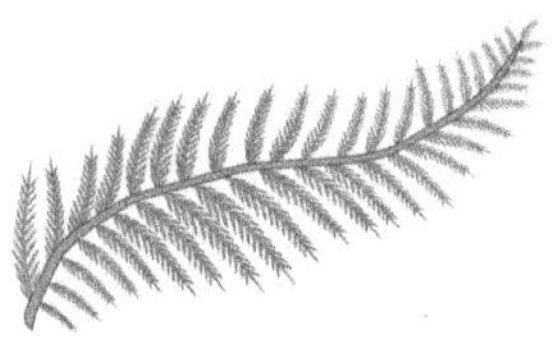

What if someone walked up to you today and said, "You are perfect", would you believe them?

What if another person walked over to you and said, "You have done everything so well" would you believe them?

What if multiple people kept saying the same things over and over to you? Would you believe it?

My hunch is there would be a moment of reflexive --- but, but, but...

WHY?!

Why does the voice of doubt, guilt, regret, sorrow, shame hold more power over the way you see yourself than anything nice someone says?

People are helping you see more of yourself.

You deserve the experience of trying and making a mistake. Choices that you later may regret but had to make no matter what. It was your best at that moment! And, only you need to approve of you. Guilt and shame are the currency of someone else's disapproval.

For your own heart and wellness, please give yourself the gift of receiving the kind messages.

Let the words of acceptance wash over you. Feel them into your body. You are perfect just as you are.

You are doing your best.
You can make a mistake and still be loveable.
You can have regrets and still be amazing!
Wrap yourself in a big hug and know you are a miracle.

Rekindled Value

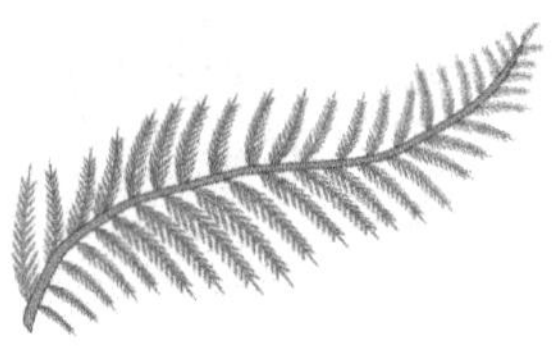

This exchange is confusing for us both
I once gave of my time freely
I pause
I ask, what is it you are asking of me
How would you like to be supported here

You pull back
What do you mean
We are friends

I know this is confusing for us both.

We are friends
And at this moment, I am acting as more
You need guidance
Coaching
Direction
I am holding a container
Facilitating
Healing

Again I ask
How would you like me to support you
Still a bit startled
You wonder

I ponder

How does a healing practitioner go from
Free support
To honor their own needs

I, too, have responsibilities.
People counting on me
My time is not free

I am honoring my value.
My energy is asking me to firm up my borders
There is a cost to free services
An imbalance when the tables tipped

How do we navigate the discomfort of
New boundaries
Clear communication
Unearthing expectations
How do we hold both
Friendship and Professional support

This bundle of tangled lines
Has begun to unravel
I know it isn't obvious
I want to apologize
I want to shrink back
Do it the usual way

I am sorry for not establishing direction
From our first interaction

I have changed

Grown
Developed

I am rekindling the light
Of my value
My time matters
My skills are helpful.

Every time I step into that space
The space of this is no longer a friendly catch up
I am present to the need

We both have needs
Consent
Decision

So again I ask you
How would you like me to support you

Risktakers

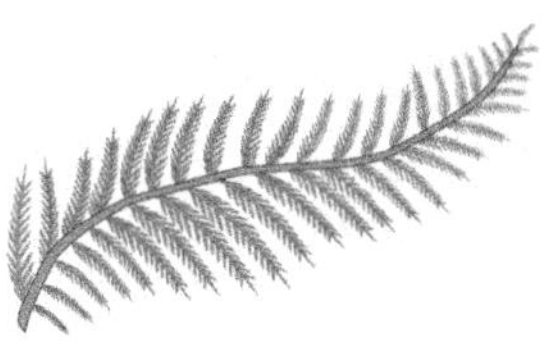

I want to take a moment to thank the risk-takers in the world. The ones who jump when I am still taking steps. It's not that they are braver, insane, or less thoughtful. I know it is just the opposite. It comes from a deep place of knowing that the most significant risk of all is not taking one.

It wounds our soul more to be idle than to leap.
It wounds our integrity more to deny our yearnings than to leap.
It wounds our relationships more to pretend we are happy than to leap.
It wounds the world's health for one to hide their magic than to leap.
It wounds self-trust to not go after your desire than to leap.
It wounds the inspiration that came through you to pause than to leap.
It wounds the audience that believes in you than to leap.

The wounding comes from denying that you are a risk-taker. To lay low, under the radar, to blend into the world that doesn't even appreciate the bend.

Not everyone is meant for risk. The non-risk-takers are the balance. They are the ones who applaud your efforts. Who can see the calculations of your decision, support your madness, and say, "someday I wish to be just like him." As hard as it may be for some people to *understand* a risk-taker, they still appreciate their fervor.

Rituals

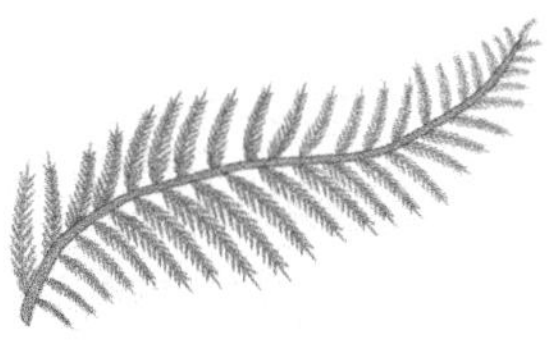

I'm pondering the balance of rituals in a modern lifestyle. There may not always be time to create a ceremony.

Rituals are available every second of our lives.

It's as simple as drip coffee to French press.

Whole tea or loose leaf
Appreciating the notable differences in between.

When I make drip coffee, it brews quantity.
It's also an automatic process that I don't pay much attention.

Whereas with a french press, I'm keen on the whole process and engage my senses.

Today I slowed from my "gotta do's" to "what I want to do." I brewed coffee in my French press and relished the aromas, sounds, and beauty of it steeping.

I thought over my list and prioritized my day.

Let go of any sense of urgency.

Slow brewing coffee can be symbolic of quiet brewing life.

As I desire to have a more developed flavor to living, it asks me to slow my process and engage more fully in each moment.

Sensitive

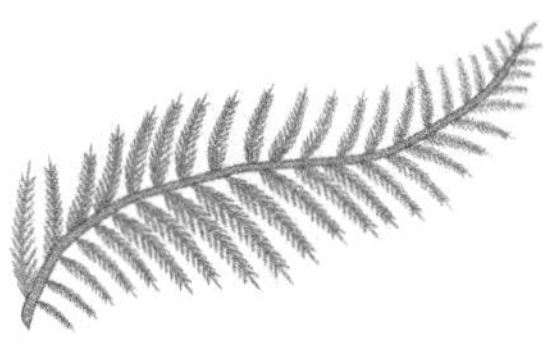

Being a sensitive person comes with perks and drawbacks.

I cry a lot
I am intense
I feel most everything
I don't pretend when something is off
I may not always *know* what I am sensing
I detect subtleties in conversations
I falter with boundaries from time to time
I pray nightly for the end of suffering
I try to help as often as possible, sometimes to my
 detriment
I let in everyone and slowly learn to be more discerning
I see beauty where most avert their eyes
I see the pain behind smiles
I trust that each person can handle their growth
I try to ask better questions, fewer assumptions
I used to build walls; now I am creating loving
 boundaries.

Shadow Trainer

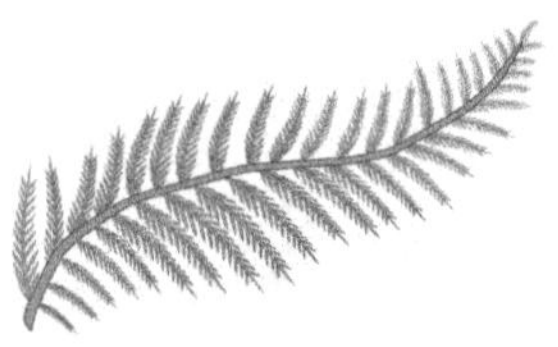

There is no more extraordinary teacher of shadow work than number 45. Suppose we aren't using this time to elevate our consciousness. Call back our projections, and see beyond the injustices. We are missing a remarkable opportunity to heal the core of trauma.

Right now, it's a mess. It is confusing and terrifying, and it seems counterintuitive to trauma healing. We are in the in-between of what can no longer be a part of our collective and how to create something different.

Our very existence birthed through violence.
Who hasn't been traumatized?
How do we know how to do something in a new way, if what we repeatedly see is old?

We are all given a chance to move beyond the pain. It starts with admitting that it is here and we can't make it all better. We can slowly stop reliving it through our stories, thoughts, and actions.
We are more than our hurts.
We can begin to envision a world where trauma isn't the first response to overwhelming circumstances.

A world where we make decisions from responding, not reacting.

A world where we are mindful, patient, aware.

A world where mistakes are forgiven.

A world where we focus on the present and not keep trying to make the past better.

A world where we take responsibility for ourselves and stop blaming other people.

A world where every second is a reminder of the preciousness of life.

A world where we are aware of the endless miracles great and small.

It isn't easy. It isn't an overnight fix. It is in fact, a path to help change the world.

This message moved through me. I do not believe I know how to change the world. I want to honor the energy that wished to express itself through my vessel.

Shallow Breath

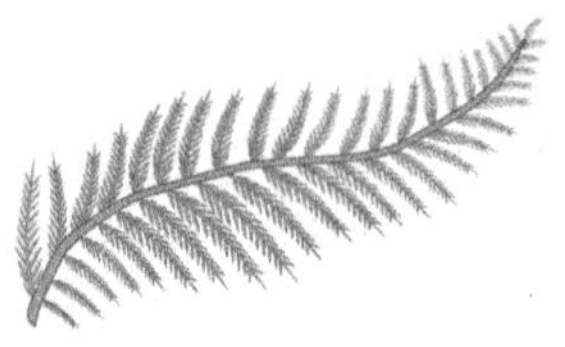

When shallow breath
It leaves the mind meek
Follow the wind to crests
Of hearts pleat

Chasing tomorrows
Being thought today
No end in the array

When shallow breath
Turn to hearts beat
Ripple in the rhythm
Paves the street of now

When shallow breath
Echoes in the cosmos
Sit still
For the guests
That pray your name
No thoughts will bring
You peace
Until you've cleared your silo
Through deepened breaths.

Shame

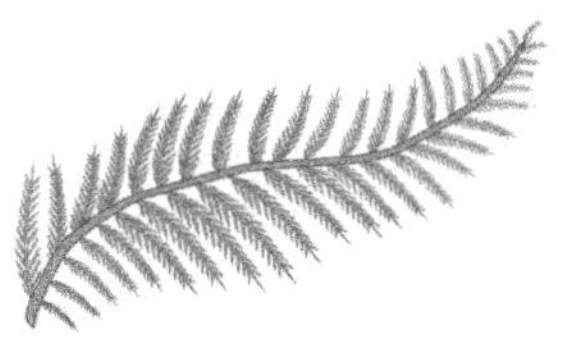

Shame
Is a cave
Dark
Dank
Isolating
A ray of light peaks through
Too far to follow
You stay in the hallow
Of false beliefs
Voices long passed
This self-created hell
Is gooey and sticky
Hard to navigate
Harder still to leave
You believe you belong here
That the world could never accept you
You're tainted
Broken
Unworthy of grace
Love or understanding
You are far too shameful to be seen
How does this serve you?
Do not buy the illusion
You will lose far more than what can be gained here
Love

Peace
Growth
Experiences
Self-trust
Trusting others
Hearing your own heart
The only thing that shame can offer you is
MISERY
It's not who you are
It's a distraction for control
It's not YOU
The feelings are real
And
ANd
AND
You can let them go!
Let shame know who you are
You are human
You are doing your best
You are not your mistakes
You are learning
You are growing
You own your shit
Once you are here owning your shit
Shame loses it's grip
You are free!

Shell

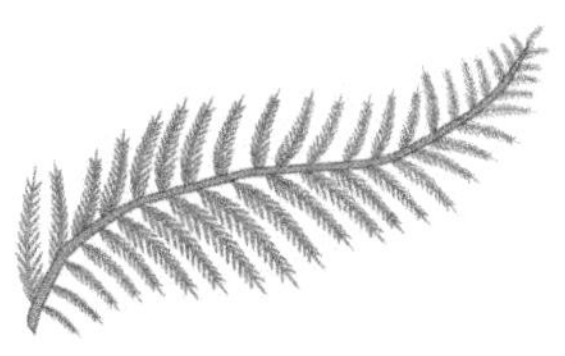

What if we were all stripped of our outer shell
Normal
We are all bare
How would we then judge or compare
Ourselves to another
Would they be too bony
To bright
Would we look away in fright
Too real to handle
The dismantling of judgment
Why does one judge
Feel more superior too
Better than
It's their shadowland
A place deep inside
That one believes is truth
The shadowland
It is an abandoned place
Lost in the depths
Of being seen by its true face
It sneaks
Hides
Undermines
The highest and brightest
Not out of malice

But from fear
You see
At some time in one's life, they believed that someone
or something was
Smarter
Thinner
Stronger
Better
Brighter
Truer
Then they
They made the comparison mean something about
themselves
Feeling inferior on the exterior of their world
They judge
Condemn
Shame
Blame
Maim
Name it as another's fault
Problem
Persecution
It's a delusion
The big illusion of life
There isn't another out there
That carries your light
It's your birthright
Pull back the projection
The separation
And allow the truth to set your free
You are no different than me

Sitting

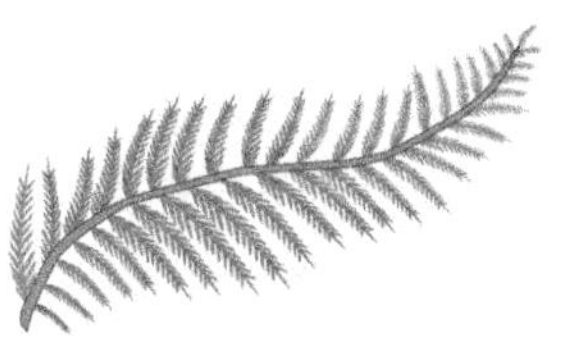

I mean, is there any conditioning worse than being told
how to go to the bathroom?

When and where it's acceptable to pee.

How many times a day is "Normal." (We are judging
the frequency of bowel movements?)

Which way to wipe!
Come on!
Let me be my wipe-r for a girls' gotta wipe the way a
girls' gotta wipe.

To squat or not to squat --- Cheers to those who can
stand!

You're a rebel, and I love you.

Soften

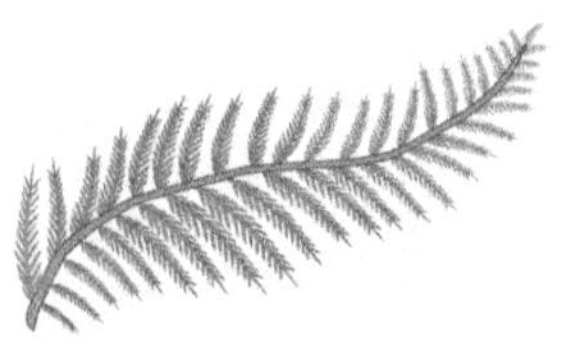

Respecting the inverse choice
To soften in adversity
Allow the ballads to
Slough
Fray
Meld into a new
Form

Opening the vulnerable
Core
During waves
Of storms

The warrior
Learned her strength
Came not from
Sword
Lowering her head
Taking a knee

It's in humility
We stand amongst
The canopy

Sometimes

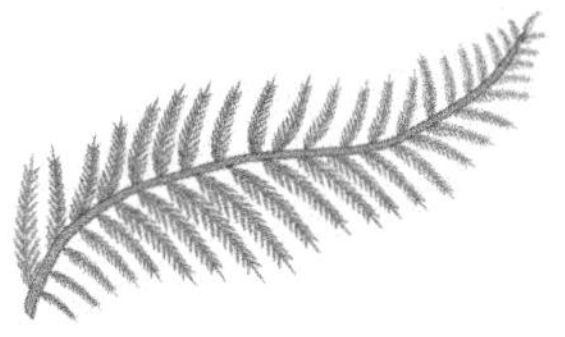

Sometimes...
Sometimes the gentle yell.
Sometimes the weak fight.
Sometimes the tired soar.
Sometimes the empath blocks.
Sometimes the intuitive ignores.
Sometimes the kind is mean.
Sometimes the love is fierce.
Sometimes the graceful stammer.
Sometimes the brave bow.
Sometimes the confident hide.
Sometimes the scared flee.
Sometimes the rain stops.
Sometimes the curtain drops.
Sometimes the sun sets.
Sometimes we try again.
Only to find
Sometimes we had it right along.

Soul I know you

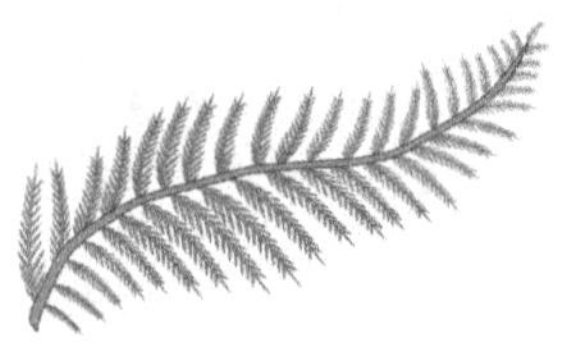

Look in the mirror
Past your messy hair
Wrinkles
Voices of old
Keep looking girl
The sheathes around your heart
Look for your potent self
Behind your eyes
The quiet
Loving
Unconditional
Part of your being
Your soul
Wait until you're invited
To step through the door
Of false beliefs
Folklore
Bow to her
Show your reverence
Devotion
To living from her voice
Keep looking girl
As she leads you to the cosmos
Every damn thing you need
She has kept safe and whole

She is your caretaker
Keep looking girl
Until you fall away
The blank space
The void isn't to be avoided
Breathe
Soften your gaze
Allow the form to take shape
The form behind the
Smoke and mirrors
This is you
There is no judging
No fixing
Worry has fallen
Fear can't penetrate this place

Steady Heart

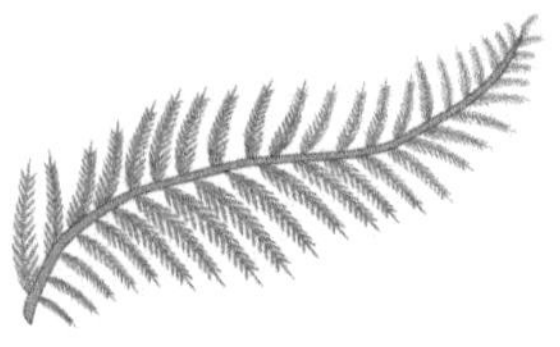

They say the human heart beats 100,000 times a day.
That is 100,000 opportunities.
Isn't that a marvel?
100,000 times to choose
100,000 to amend
100,000 to experience

This morning I observed in between the beats. The sun is playing peek-a-boo with the clouds. The snow isn't sure it wants to stay, so it breezes through with flurries. The ground is cool enough to hold the flurries until the sun peeks through. The outer nature is a reflection of events taking place within me.

I am ebbing and flowing through many different emotions. Some have a stronger pull than others. Many memories are floating through; I am playing peek-a-boo, with long passed times. Yet, the feelings are as fresh as the flurries. Times of a house bustling with little feet drumming on the wood floors, giggles and squeals as the dogs chase them; they wanted to play, too. They were all having a moment, I the happy spectator. They are taking in all of the bliss.

Now the house is creaking and cool. The only drum hums from the furnace. The doors of each room stay shut. Age has quieted the squeals, and we are in the turning of a new season.

The littles are now preparing for their next phase of life and growth. The eldest dog is weakening and drools, more than I enjoy. I look at her greying face and thank her for using all of her strength to still stand beside me—so many years of companionship and loyalty. I wonder whether she will still be here in the fall when her best friend leaves for college.

My eyes dampening at the thought of how many heart-beats we shared, these times in our home and world, quickened my breath. I try not to seize up but soften. To keep my heart supple, my eyes open, my gaze long. I want to remember all of the moments between the moments. The ease and the struggle. The raucousness and calm. The newness of life and its inevitable end. There are many beats between these poles of existence. It is in the in-between we learn to deepen.

Stretch

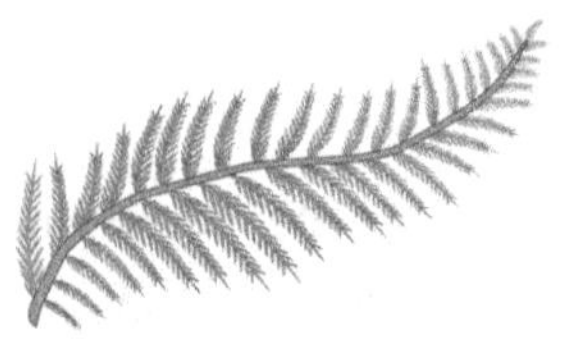

How long will you hang on?
I do not know

How long will you continue to stretch?
I do not know

Are you aware that stretching isn't the same
As growing?

Why is it you deny your soul to grow?
I thought the stretch was its growth

Your soul has been stretching beyond this time and
space
Karma is a real place
It clings to the evolution
Of a soul's eternal revolution

Your soul isn't interested in the trivial
Nor does it head the sounds of those who revile
Its authority
Your soul is your northern light
The guide of the quest

The ego will reject

The soul's quest
Disrupt what you digest

Do not relent
Head or tolerate
Become dispirited

Invite the false self to tea
Open the door to your psyche
Relieve your spirit
Of conformity

Succeeding with Soul

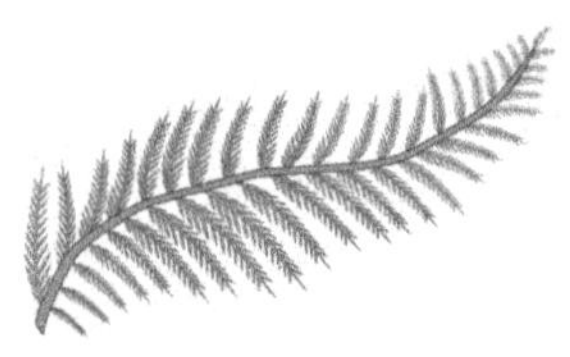

Is it a failure to not be relatable?
Is it a failure to not like domesticity?
Is it a failure to stand for what you believe in?
Is it a failure to need to eat but not want to cook?
Is it a failure to look nice and have zero interest in shopping?
Is it a failure to try your best and fall face first, time and time again?
Is it a failure to cry all the time and feel your feelings deeply?
Is it a failure to live from the strongest signal you can at any moment?
Is it a failure to be entirely devoted to something no one else can see or touch?

By what standard do we measure failure?
What is success?
Where does the soul fit in all of this?

Most of the things I deem as a failure are ego-driven.
Lies that I fight with all of the time.
Stories that I took on as my own.
Conditioning I used to rely on to survive.

How can one live according to the urgings of their soul
in modern society?
How can one thrive by following the guidance of their
soul?
Is it irresponsible to listen to our soul's urgings?
Is it irresponsible to live by your unique rhythm?

Very little I do because I am supposed to, or should be
doing it, is satisfying.

My life doesn't line up with the 9-5, happy homemaker
model when I work from the soul level.
Most of my day is hard to plan, anticipate from this
place.
I seem unreliable or disrespectful.
Isn't it disrespectful to not listen to your soul?

Support

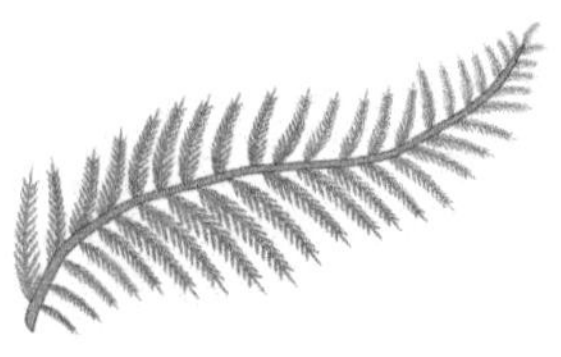

There are few achievements in life done solo
If not asked for, yet given
Not always by humans
The winds, Earth, Rain, Sun
Four-legged, two-leggeds, microscopic ones
Always we are supported
With loving care
Keep your heart open
Vision clear
And allow what is meant to guide you---step
beside you.

Survivors

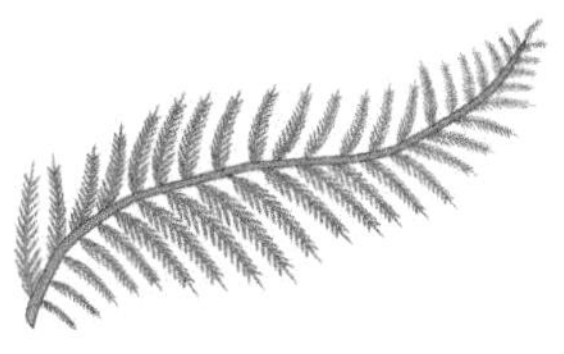

We are all survivors
Birth
Adolescence
Through wars
Divide
Opposition
and hate.

We are all survivors
The war that you live through may not have been in
Kuwait
But waged in your own heart
Thoughts
Beliefs
A silent battle
Between you
And the nameless face on the street

We are all survivors
Of judgments
Criticisms
Shrewdness
Hard hearts

Ignorance

Given this one chance
This one planet
This next breath, if we're lucky

We're all survivors
How are we going to use our battle skills to become
thrivers?

Repair the divide
Bridge the gap
Lay our heads
On the great mother's lap
Be one with them all
No more separation
From the great fall

This our rebirth
Lay hands upon
The soil
Laying to rest
The toil
Of unconsciousness

Suspended Memories

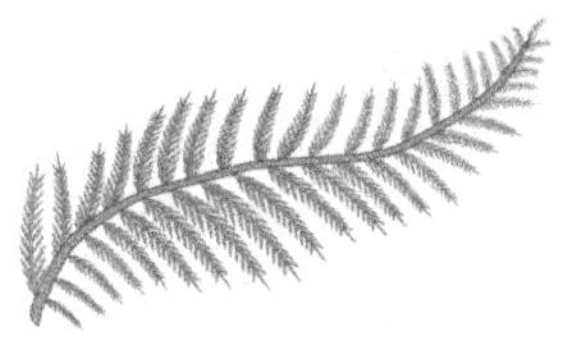

Suspended memories
Bobbing comparisons
Of what was
And what I thought it was supposed to be
An outsider peering into the memory
My heart weeps for the lasts
Cuddles
Books
Giggles
Sing a longs
And the endless "why?"

All the times, I said, "one more minute."
"Not now"
"We will do it tomorrow."

Shiny slides occupied by a new family
Why's replaced with "I know."
Swings swaying to new memories
I thought we had infinite time

I see them pushing off from the shore.
I check the ship for holes, leaks, signs of danger
They're safe
It's my heart that's calculating risks

These moments in time
segments strewn together
We prepared for the now
But I didn't see it coming
Busy with the fascination of youthful Innocence
Now hurrying for adulthood seriousness
I let out a sigh

I want more time
More cuddles
Long summer days of nothing planned
Meandering in fields of daisies

With sun stroked locks
Dirty knees
And momma, just five more minutes, please!

Now I'm the one asking for more time
Don't rush
Stay awhile
Tell me about your days
What interests you these days

My children
Are a vast sky
Ever shifting and changing
I can't hold onto them any more than a cloud
I watch
I ponder
I appreciate

Reach into my heart for a new thread

Sewing another segment into
Our history.

Talking

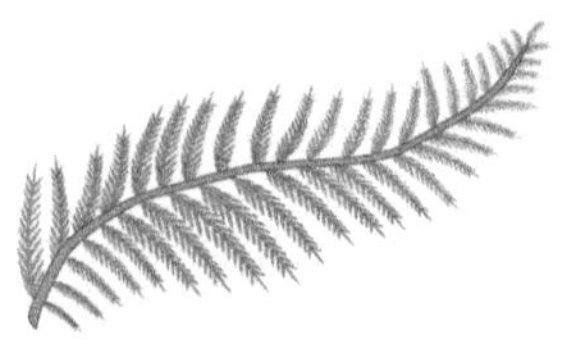

I am not you
I don't speak the way you do
I don't think the way you do
I don't care about the same things as you

Why do you grasp my voice?
And tell me how to be

Why do you suffocate me?
Stripping my dignity

Is this the best you want for me
Was this what they did to you

Don't you see this is repeated
Injury
Generation to Generation

When did the silenced in our line retire their
Veneration

It's becoming to speak your truth
The truth changes as one ages
It's relevance in all its phases

Do you not take pleasure in
Tonal soiree

Candor
A symphony
Evolution
Retiring
Antiquity

Tapestry of our Love

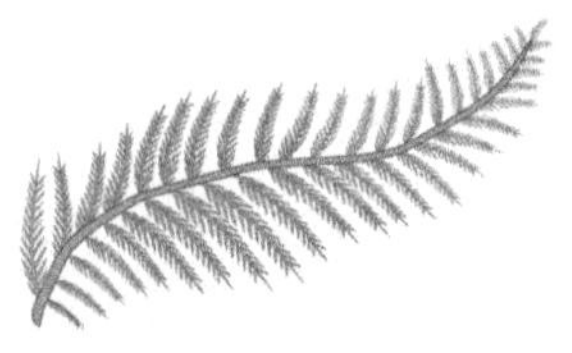

The tapestry of our love
Came with missed stitches
Loops around
Squares lined in gold
Patterns repeating
Mothering your scars
Our growing pains
They informed me

The tapestry of our love
It tells a story of triumph
Solitude
Strife
Forgiveness
and humor

Woven with what we had
When your clock struck zero
I gathered our tapestry
I laid it on top of my newborn son
Stretching over my daughter
To the last son

The tapestry of our love
Lays at the foot of the family tree

New stories
Threads
Colors
Added daily
Tended by this generation

The original story told
With missed stitches
Were no accident
Invitation to pause
Moments to linger
Learn
Begin again

The tapestry of our love
A remembering of
Speckled history gathered
For the lineage
Intricate illustrations
Of devotion
Living beyond a knotted thread

Textured Living

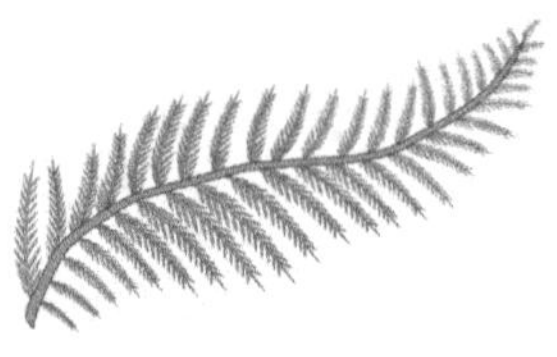

How do I stay soft in hard times?
How do I allow when faced with waves of anxiety?
How do I open my home when there's a threat afoot?
How do I protect the children?

Who am I when I'm not in control?
Who am I as a citizen when nothing makes sense?

How to love when I feel brittle
How to stay with softness when my edges feel
 hardened

I've heard "we are made for these times."

I have another inkling,
These times were made because of me.
Choices that led to this moment
Unconscious consumption
Ignorance
Denial
All to protect what is mine.

My home
My land
My food

My family
My career
My money

Me, mine, me, mine

All the while, the Earth that I walk upon
Softly asks, "What of us?"

Too busy to hear
Too busy to feel
Too busy to look
Too busy to wonder

Me, mine, me, mine

Again she asks, "What about us?"

In these times, there is no other place to look than within.

The time of blame, over
The time of denying, ending
The time of fantasy, over
The time of helplessness, ending
The time of overconsumption, over

What about us?
What about We?
Who are we in times of unity?
How will we come back to the Community?
What are we going to do about the state of affairs?

WE are in a State of emergence-Y
WE are Awakening to our dependency of US
WE are walking out of our masks
Our illusions
Our dream

We are being asked, "What about us?"
Who will we be when we complete our emergence-Y?

Thanksgiving

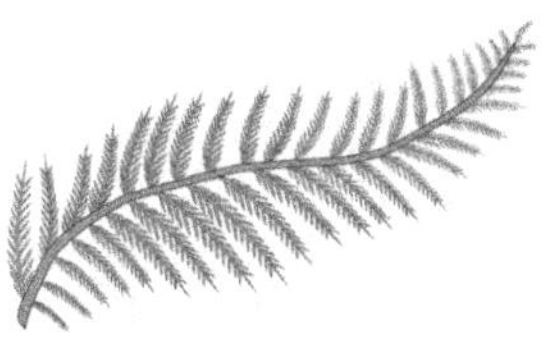

I would be fibbing if I said that holidays are times of ease for me. Each year comes with a different nuance of remembering and anticipation. As I look around our table at the empty chairs, death or proximity has kept guests from our table. There are more chairs I would like to add for the friends that are family to me.

I have this inner struggle to balance a well-worn tradition with the desire to pioneer a new one.

This year we are trying something different with the family. We are going to a nice restaurant to celebrate Thanksgiving and then back for desserts at my in-laws. Our time together is what we treasure most, and the hours of labor in the kitchen are beginning to wear on the host and hostess. It was fun to discuss and collaborate on what was most important for each of us also plan a new way of celebrating.

I lit a candle for my ancestors and family that have crossed over this morning—honoring the delicious recipes that only they could make, the richness of their wisdom and conversations. Memories that are treasured and always bring a smile to my heart.

Blessings were sent to my friends and family, with gratitude for all the love they give freely and abundantly to our family.

Most importantly, honoring my new perspective that we share more similarities than differences with others we know or encounter—keeping my heart soft, open, giving.

May today be filled with celebrating in a way that feels right to you. Your belly is full, home warm, and heart full. <3

This moment is reflective of where I am in my own life and growth. Every day, I am pioneering new ways that align with who I choose to be. Fine-tuning here or grand excavating over there. Either way, they each have their level of intensity. The more delicate tuned I become, the more attention and precision is needed, which can be pretty frightening. The same can be said for upheaving a significant belief or pattern in my life!

The Awakened

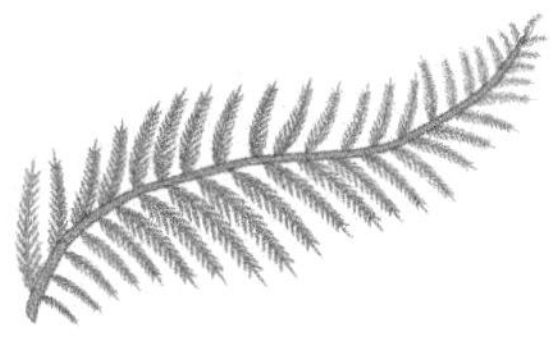

You've been here a long while
Everything still looks the same
But now
Now everything feels differently
What happened?
Why is this happening?

How can things seem the same
And yet,
They are completely changed.
What happened?
Why is this happening?

Everything feels aggressive
Assertive
And you
You sweet one are tender

Like a shoot just breaking through the surface
Reaching
Stretching
Warming in the light

Why is the world you've always known
Suddenly

Without warning or cause
A harsh place for you to be

Welcome to your awakening
The safety of ignorance is
Slowly
Steadily
Falling
Falling
Falling
Away

Will it always be so hard?
So dense
Intensely
Acutely
Achingly
Difficult
That depends on you
It sounds trite to say
Do not resist this
Do not try to turn back
It's hopeless to do so

It seems like the wise thing to do
Pretend this isn't happening
No one knows that it's
Taking place for you, but you

The difficulties you are experiencing
Are causal
Not permanent
The more you can soften

The more enjoyable
The awakening can be
Not that it will be

You see the stripping that is happening
Is the removal of comfort
Certainty

Where you are heading
There is no ability to hang on
Attach yourself
You are learning how to glide
Sail
Fall in

The updrafts of life will keep you
Moving
Gliding
Edging along

Let these winds take you
To the place you've yet
To be
Discovery...

The Pieces

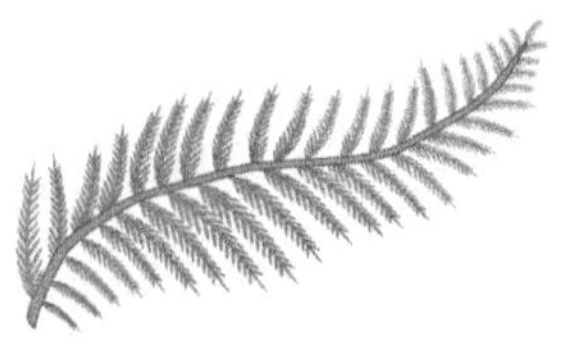

I want to feel my brokenness
I want my brokenness to be seen
Numb for too long
My world has fallen apart
I'm sitting here with pieces
Shell shocked
Shivering
Dampened from the inside out

How can this be
I did everything right
I obeyed the rules ways of society
I paid my taxes
Tended the children
I looked after my elders

How can this be
I held on tightly to what I was told would make me a
good member of society.

How can this be, you ask?
Let me explain

You followed the rules of a ruler who had lost
their way.

You obeyed the laws and rules written by sickened souls.
You were being led by those who stopped leading themselves.
You were obeying a script that was penned out of self-indulgence.
How can men be trusted whose thirst for material gain comes from the blood of another brother?

How can this be
It's called the dream
Most humans never awaken from the dream

While this hurts
And you are scared

I encourage you to keep feeling
To keep asking questions
To listen to your instincts
Trust only the way of good and just

If you worry, you'll fall back asleep
If you worry, you may begin dreaming again
Leave yourself a key
Something to remind you of this moment
Something that will keep you on your journey
You are the dreamer within the dream

The Power of Yes

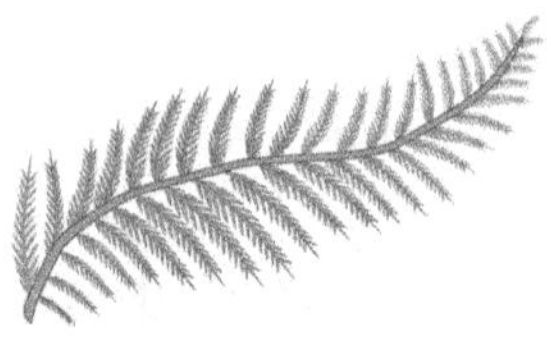

Dear Current Self,

Why are you resistant right now, this moment? Why are you angry, tired, and stressed. What is it about this moment in your only life that has you troubled? In a year from now, looking back, what will you wish you had done differently? With new information, growth, and insights, I am sure you would have let this one go; said ok to have a friend over and not worried or been bothered by how much the dogs were barking; how tired your body was feeling, or how bad your head hurts from all the noise. You can choose to see this one differently. You can choose gratitude to have a home from which to host. Your children have good friends and happy memories because you've said yes. When they found you, the animals were in need, and you said yes to them. You live in tight quarters with big hearts and a small home.

No one is at fault. It just needs love and affection to be seen and felt. Not the negativity that usually comes with stress or burden. Give thanks, be merry, and know that your life is everything you have chosen it to be. Everything in this house is because you have said yes. If yesterday's yes's do not serve you today, then it is time to say yes to something new! Not anguish or anger, make a new choice, one that is right with your heart and mind. one that will bring peace today. And if you are lucky enough to face tomorrow, you again can choose a new yes! Always, it's a choice that belongs to you.

With love,
Future Self

The Runner

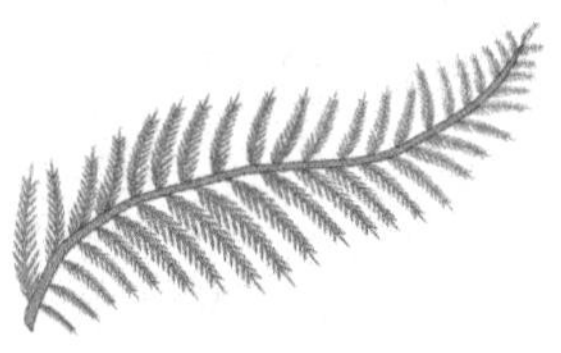

You often say, "I don't know how your brain works."
I know that I hurt you today.
My brain says, "Great; now you've ruined everything.
He doesn't want to be with you anymore."
Etc. etc. etc....
I'll spare you the whole string of inner commentary.
This commentary, you see, is where my beliefs live
I believe these thoughts and want to run!
So I say to you, "This relationship isn't working."
I'm not good for you.
"You can do better than me."
I am still learning how to have a normal response to conflict.
But I go to extremes
How can I be honest with my feelings?
Does what I am feeling come from a false narrative?
A record that keeps skipping.
I hit the rib of "I am not good for you."
Put on my running shoes,
Head for the door.

What stops me from walking through?
The runner can only find one shoe.

Tired

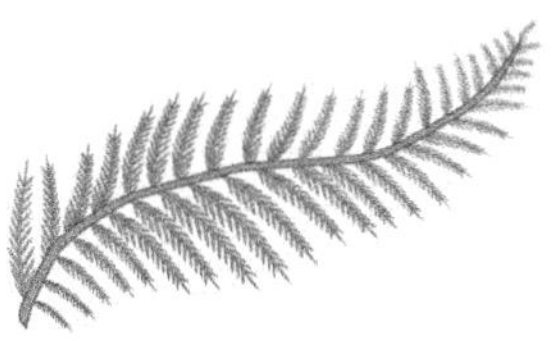

Tired

Maybe today you see an independent
Strong
Fiery
Passionate
Woman

I'm tired

Tired of telling myself
I can do it all
Be all things
All the time
To all people
I need to be strong

I'm tired

Of passing by a sunrise
To hurry
Plan
Achieve
Master

I'm tired

Hearing the pressing urgency of others
Needs
Wants
Over my own
Pushing the clock back
Whence more

I'm tired

Battling my demons
Being scorched by the dragons
Not waiting for the unicorn

As time wore on

I became more interested in
Creating legends
and
Stopped chasing myths
began
Using my voice
First to myself
Then to the world

Honoring my no
Listening for my big fat YES
Not always in my chest, but my belly

I regained my energy
My clarity
My dignity

And integrity

Today when I'm tired, I rest
No longer guilty
My priorities are back on top
Over being dutiful

It's my life too
No longer tired
Or choosing others
Before what is best for me

I am here to write my own history
Leave a legacy
And create prophecy
Being dreamed into reality
After my bones decay

I am creating a new way
For the woman line
Of my family
Honoring
Their sacred mission
Not become enslaved to conformity

It's not the norm to be exhausted
It's not the norm to be doing it all
It's not the norm to be a superhero
It's not the norm to sacrifice happiness
For one more errand on the list

Today I Grieve

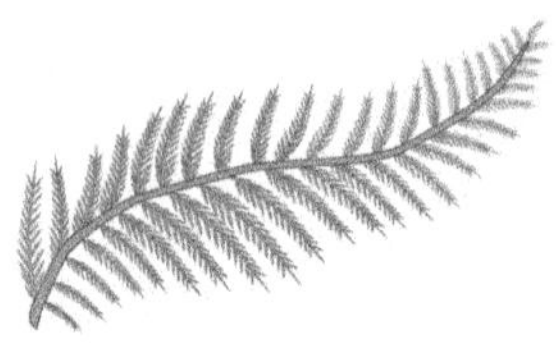

As I allow the trickling in of Joy
A tide of grief is rising
I have to wrestle this feeling like a gigantic Alligator
To see into its eyes
The eyes of grief travel through millennia
No beginning or end
The timeless suffering
Is incredulous to sit with
How can this be century after century
Harm to another
For the varied skin color
Taking Lands
Lives
Dreams
All ashes in the sand of our shores
This sand can't be stored
The grief must be unleashed
Felt by the masses
Before we can begin to release our defenses
To every eye we see
Taking responsibility
The only division is the one we believe
Differences aren't to be judged or assumed
There is no shame in the deed
The way one lives in a house or tree

On a boat in the deep sea
What difference does it make to me!
The space around my heart is cracking, peeling
Allowing the lies I've been told
Or sold to me
In order to feel above or better
Than someone else
All this fucking privilege
It disgusts me
When I can eat whatever I want
But she can't feed her babies
Who am I do have more
Unwilling to do the labor of tough chores
That she must do
No choice
No decision
Only division
By our democracy
I don't have the solution
I do have a voice
An ambition
To leave this world better than I found it
If not by my work
Deeds
Or legacy
By the heart that beats
The breath I weave
I can choose to feel the grief
The misdeeds
Of my ancestors
My society
I can choose to be kind
To all I see

And believe the best
In Spite of what I see
For humanity's sake
Someone deserves to be believed in
Even if it's only my dream

Triangles

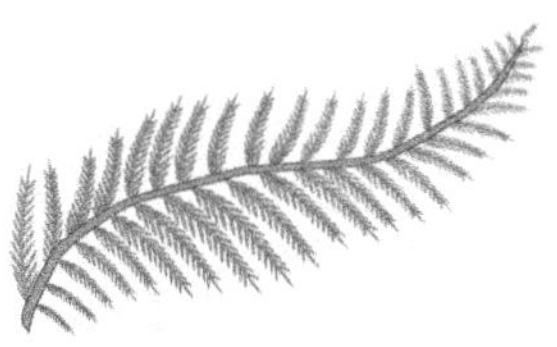

Last night, I revisited patterns I thought were healed and transformed—, particularly regarding bias. I have a villain story about my mother. A story that I later placed onto my spouse and daughter. They all share similar traits in the way we relate to one another. I used to leave zero room for them to be who they are. I would assign them the villainous storyline, and everything they did fit in the box perfectly. I would feel satisfied that I was proven right, once again. YUK!

Once I saw the pattern, had an awareness of its plan, and began working on the healing. Restructuring has been an ongoing process for over two years.

It's painful

It's shame invoking

It's guilt-laden

I believe all of it has its place, the good, bad, and the ugly.

The truth is, it isn't who I know myself to be. I had a hard time accepting this truth when it first surfaced. Over time I can see how it has served me; I used to feel like a victim. I believed the world was unfair unsafe, and I didn't belong. It helped me to believe these things when villains were around me. Here is the punch in the gut. The villain lives

inside of me. It is one of my shadows that I projected onto others to help me see it.
Every time I blame/d another for their behavior. I was trying to wake myself up. The projection was there because I couldn't see the behavior belonged to me!

The difficulty in the healing process is integrating. Bringing in more light and letting the shadows be known. Writing this and sharing it with you is hard. It is also healing. I have nothing to hide when it comes to the parts that create the whole. I wouldn't be honoring myself or others to pretend I am always good, light, and reverent.
I am human
I am trying to figure out what makes me tick
What works well, and what needs to be reconfigured in the Brigid landscape?

Value

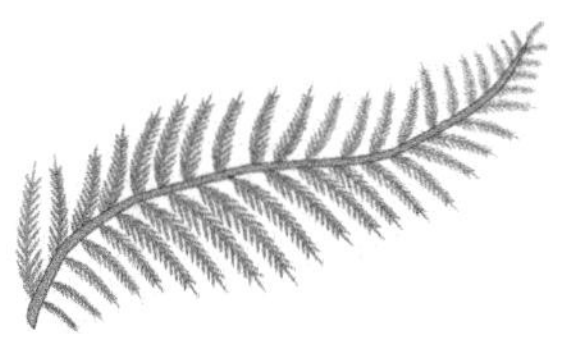

Five little letters that shape our lives
In the day to day action
If not in alignment, it creates a distraction
From the truth of our traction
Values are forward motion
In the light of our path
When we do not know if they matter
They can be debris and scatter
We hear others' values and hold them close
Knowing deep inside what matters most
ME
Not selfishly
Not selflessly
But the real ME
The me that says I live this way because it feels good
To you, me, and my neighborhood
When I live my values, not what you think I should
I can be authentic, right, solid, understood
So with the dawn of each new day
I ask myself
What are my intentions for today
Honor your values, dignity, and grace
So that life will meet you in this sacred space.

Wanted

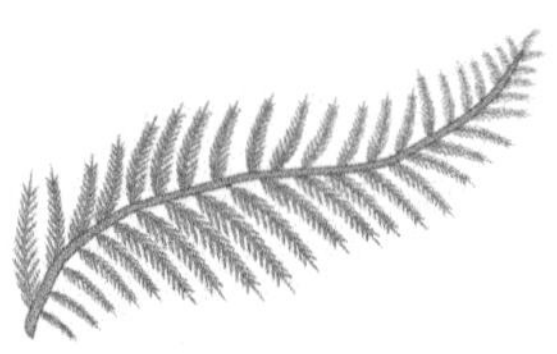

I'm not a mistake.

I am the risk my parents were willing to make to deliver me to my destiny.
Their lessons, trials, and tribulations still move through me.

I am not walking the same path.

Using their navigation to help see more of this map of life.
I know now that everything they were facing slowed in the quiet moments of their lovemaking.
They were purposeful in accepting me into their intimacy.
I was always wanted; it was part of our script that I would have heartache, stumble and slip as I made my way through insecurity.

My parents never stopped loving me.
They never looked away.
They gave birth and breadth for me to keep developing into the child of the Universe I will always be.

I didn't belong to them.

They created a pact with the creator of all; they would be the portal for my arrival.
They were brave to say yes.
I brave to entrust myself in their stead.
We all took risks, and I am to continue moving along the narrow ledge, dancing between an illusion and reality.

I am here with the capacity to create a life scribed into the code of our future children of the light.

We all Have Scars

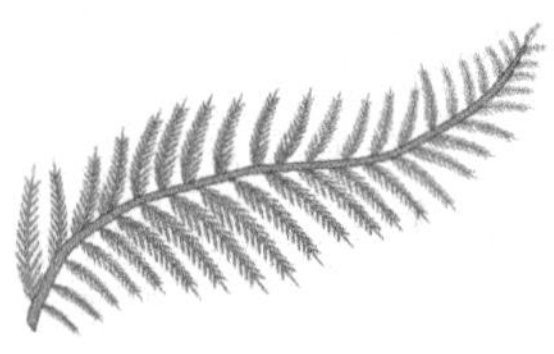

We all have scars
Let them mark time
Not brandish another's name
Do not allow these scars to deface your sense of worth
They are a passageway

Some split us from head to tail
Others stretch us
Awaiting to prevail

We all have scars
Meant to be displayed
Worn proudly in remembrance
Of what has endured
Not torture us

To liberate us
Deliver us through the canal of life

The channel that we bore
Is a marker
A signpost
For souls, we may never know
Or may never know us

Yet they walk silently
Through the trail of our scars

What's Next?

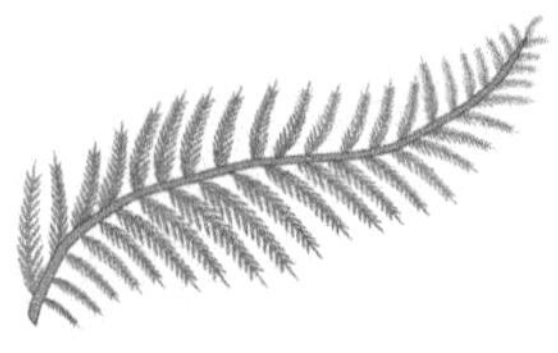

We eventually hit a space/wall/pause/time to evaluate,
Time spent in achieving this now moment.

Now what?
What's next?

I am where I wanted to be, and yet....
How is it that I still don't feel quite right?

Now what?
What's next?

Who am I here?
How do I support myself in this space of now?
Why does it feel cold and foreign?
Why do I want to push away from this place and keep going?
Where do I think I "should" be?
Why do I think anything else will be different than this?

Now what?
What's next?

Stay still

Lean in
Listen
Feel
Pulse
Breathe

There is nothing more.
There isn't a next

This is it.
Who am I here?
You are she
I am
Everything

Who I Am

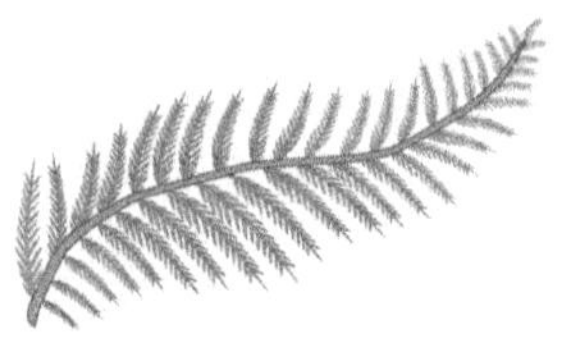

I have often wondered, Who am I?
That question serves to hasten madness
Dredging up everything, I perceive myself as lacking

To ask who I am?
Implies I don't know

I know who I am
The more accurate question is what do I do with this
knowledge.

Who I am

I am a deep river

I can become cold and distant on the surface of
anything;
Observing
Conversing
Hugging

I am steady

I take my time with life
I find life has value beyond what I can sense

I am a traveler from far away

I am here to mend health into my ancestry

I am carrying a sacred seed for humanity

I am infinite

I am warmth

I am nature

I am multiverse

I am arriving

Witnesses

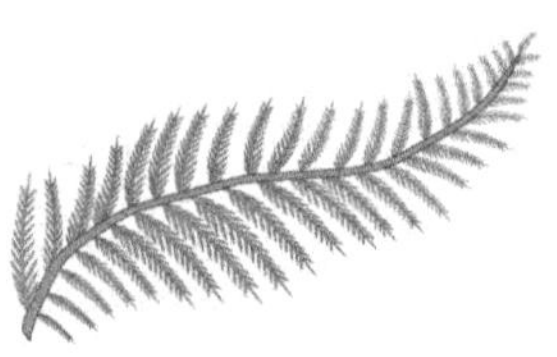

While waiting in line, we noticed a girl with soft dark curls standing in the cart. She was in the top portion where her legs were supposed to slide through. Not the large bottom cart section. Everything in me wanted to rush and stand there to catch her.

Instincts...

Are they right?

My daughter turned towards me and said, "Mom, not your kid. Not your problem."

Buuuuttt, all the reasoning was about to pour forth, and she said, "look."

An elder sister reached for the young one. The young girl clawed at her sister's face and snarled. I felt a chuckle well up. Why? Isn't this "bad behavior?"

The elder sister stayed present to the young girl and quietly spoke with the gentleness of a butterfly wing. Each word was sweeping over the younger one. After a bit, the younger one began to reach her sister and ask to be held.

I'm still staring, unable to break my gaze from this scene. The elder one began carrying her sister around the store, covering her in kisses. They were both giggling—kisses on the younger ones' cheeks forehead. Laughter abounding. She just loved on her as quickly as she spoke.

After a few minutes, the younger one asked to go back in the cart and sat happily with her legs through the holders.

I am reminded by the elder teenage sister's actions that you couldn't go wrong offering more love, not less.

She was grace in action. I left wiser for not rushing to "do something," instead, I headed my daughter's instinct to be there witnessing.

It wasn't easy, but so much richness would have been missed between the sisters. You never know who is watching and how it can change the shape of a moment.

More love, not less is a wise sentiment by Matt Khan.

Womb Legislation

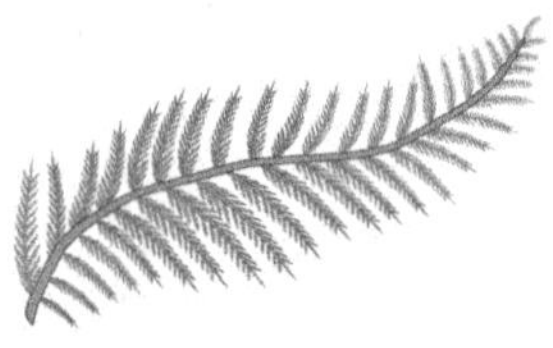

I'm angry
I'm sad
I'm tired
I'm ready to start a revolution

My revolution looks like this...

I won't spend my energy condemning the system.

I won't feed fears

I won't accept defeat.

I won't buy into any permanence.

I will regroup
I will change my focus
I will call on our ancestors
I will offer forgiveness
I will give my fears to God
I will pray through

I will put all my faith and energy into the change I want to be in the world.

The world I most want to live in fosters; Empathy
Understanding
Persistence
Patience
Trust
Faith
Collaboration
Power

The power structures are crumbling because anything built outside of ourselves that dominant, oppresses, and controls another, are NOT sustainable.

I believe we are changing.

Change is painful.
Change is confusing.
Change can feel like a disaster.

Just ask the Earth....

It's not over; it's begun

The awakened have choice
The awakened need to keep raising their frequency
The awakened keep eyes forward, hearts open
Our power comes from within
Stay the course of yOUR rising

Women's Day

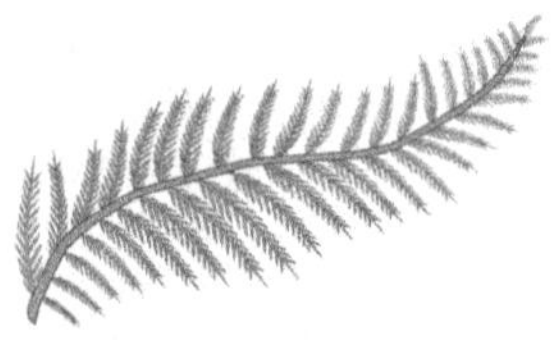

What an incredible time in history
To be me
Changing patriarchy
History
Rhetoric
Divide

I take each moment in stride
What an incredible time in history
To be me

Thank you to the
Mother's
Sisters
Daughters
Brothers
Courageous hearts
Freedom crusaders

Helping me to be seen as more than
A background
A breeder
Something to own
Or display

What an incredible time in history
To be me

The circles
Tribes
Talks
Prayers
Visioning
Seers

Slowly shifting the tides
Of what women are

What an incredible time in history
To be me

No longer weighted by should's
Lifted by could
Wait-n-see

What an incredible time in history
To be me

Celebrating all people who are encouraged
To go beyond the limiting definition
Of societies expectation
Of what being you
Means

About the Author

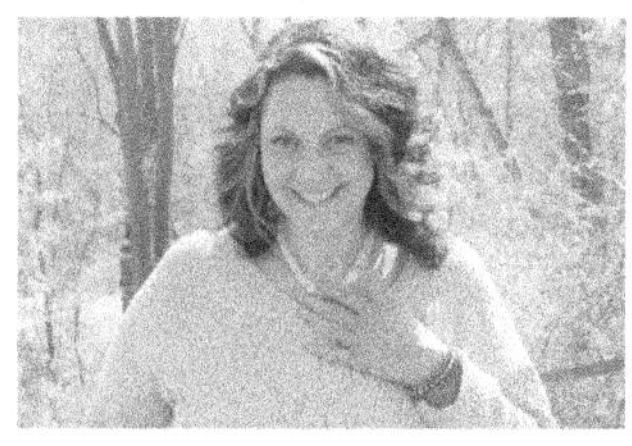

Artist, soul cartographer, dreamer and free spirit, Brigid Hopkins is a passionate student of Mother Earth and a creative visionary who loves to enrich her community and work to rejuvenate the health of our planet. As an avid apprentice of WindWork®, Reiki, shamanism, shadow work, ancestral healing, and peri/prenatal education, Brigid seeks to illuminate a path to wellbeing and help her readers pursue life-affirming health and purpose.

As the author of her debut poetry collection, Love Letters to the Earth, as well as the founder of Impermasculptures, a devotional Earth Art practice, Brigid is committed to sharing her message and inspiring her community to care for our planet and live in tandem with the natural world.

Brigid currently resides in the beautiful landscape of Northeast Ohio, the unseeded land of the Erie people, with her family. For more information, visit her website at Theclaritypath.com

www.ingramcontent.com/pod-product-compliance
Lightning Source LLC
LaVergne TN
LVHW010614100826
845148LV00014B/2960

* 9 7 9 8 9 8 5 7 3 2 4 1 2 *